Prairie-Town Boy

Also by Carl Sandburg

ROOTABAGA STORIES, PART ONE
ROOTABAGA STORIES, PART TWO
ABE LINCOLN GROWS UP
EARLY MOON
THE SANDBURG TREASURY
WIND SONG

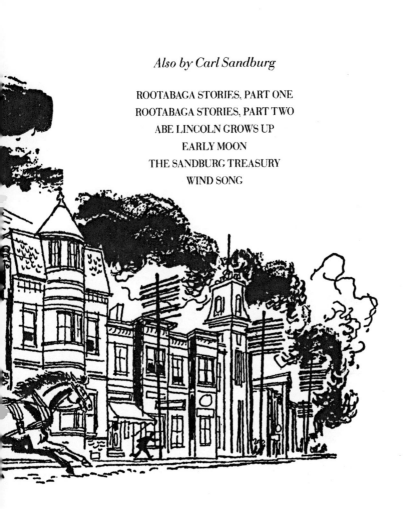

ODYSSEY CLASSIC

Prairie-Town Boy

CARL SANDBURG

Illustrated by Joe Krush

An Odyssey Classic
Harcourt Brace Jovanovich, Publishers
San Diego   New York   London

Text copyright 1953, 1952 by Carl Sandburg
Illustrations copyright © 1955 by Joe Krush
Illustrations copyright renewed 1983 by Joe Krush

Requests for permission to make copies of any part of the work should be mailed to:
Permissions Department, Harcourt Brace Jovanovich, Publishers,
Orlando, Florida 32887.

Library of Congress Cataloging-in-Publication Data
Sandburg, Carl, 1878–1967.
Prairie-town boy/Carl Sandburg; illustrated
by Joe Krush.
p.   cm.
"An Odyssey classic."
Summary: An autobiographical account of the author's
boyhood in the Midwest.
ISBN 0-15-263332-4 (pbk.)
1. Sandburg, Carl, 1878–1967 — Biography — Youth — Juvenile
literature.   2. Authors, American — 20th century — Biography — Youth —
Juvenile literature.   3. Middle West — Social life and customs —
Juvenile literature.   [1. Sandburg, Carl, 1878–1967 — Childhood and
youth.   2. Authors, American.]   I. Krush, Joe, ill.   II. Title.
PS3537.A618Z473   1990
811'.52 — dc20   90-36275
[92]
[B]

Printed in the United States of America
A B C D E

To John Carl and Karlen Paula

CONTENTS

Prologue

Prairie Town

People from New England and their children owned much of the town of Galesburg, Illinois, and set the main tone in politics, churches, schools, and colleges. Up from Kentucky and Tennessee had come English and Scotch-Irish breeds. Many Swedes had become voters and a power in politics and business. In the two and a half blocks between our house and the railroad yards the Swedes were largest in number, then the "native born," two or three Yankees, two English families, a sprinkling of Irish and Germans, and in the early 1890s a flood of Italians, some thirty men, women, and children in two houses next to the Narrow Gauge railroad tracks.

Often in the 1890s I would get to thinking about what a young prairie town Galesburg was—nearly twenty thousand people, and they had all come in fifty years. Before that it was empty rolling prairie. There was no standard pioneer cut to a regular pattern. Most of them could stand hard work and streaks of bad luck. They had broken the prairie, laid the first roads and streets, built the first schools and churches, colored the traditions of the town and country where I was born and raised. As a boy I saw some of these old-timers in their seventies or eighties, hard-bitten, grizzled, and fading. I tried in my boy mind to picture them standing where there wasn't a wall or a roof on Main Street not yet a street—no streets anywhere and no houses—looking around and deciding where to clear for the first row of houses, the Public Square, the church, the blacksmith shop, the general store—and the college to be the focus of light and hope for the youth and the coming generations. They saw their little town rise to be a place and a name where before had been silence broken only by wild-animal cries, by the recurring rains and winds.

They had left Ohio, New York, Tennessee, or Kentucky in a wagon holding family—sometimes six, eight, or ten children—and household goods. They had driven their horses over wilderness trails where often the feet of horses, the rims and spokes of wheels, tangled in underbrush. They camped where night found them and took up their journey again at daylight. Some had made part of their trip on flatboats or paddle wheel steamboats—the generation who arrived before the railroad came to Knox County in 1854.

At the time I was born, one pioneer stood out above all others in the town and county—George W. Brown, then mayor of Galesburg. A farm boy in Saratoga County, New York, he learned the carpenter's trade, and worked on the earliest railroads of the Mohawk Valley. He heard from relatives of good land cheap in Illinois, and in 1836, at twenty-one, he and his wife rode a covered wagon west for weeks on weeks while the rains came nearly every day and the wagon wheels stuck in mud and clay and had to be lifted or pried loose. In July, some nine miles from Galesburg, he traded his team of horses for an eighty of land. His wife ran the farm while he built houses. In later years, in Galesburg,

Knoxville, Henderson Grove, they pointed to houses well built by George W. Brown. He laid by what he could of his earnings while thinking and studying and experimenting with a machine to plant corn.

In the spring of 1852 he planted with his machine sixteen acres of corn for himself and eight acres for a neighbor. That year he planned and hoped to finish ten machines, and he completed only one. He sold livestock, then his last horse, for means to clinch his patents. In order to go on and produce and sell his cornplanters, he sold his farm and borrowed money at ten percent interest. In 1856 he got his shops in Galesburg going and made six hundred cornplanters and the next year a thousand. His machines spread over the Midwest during the .war years, 1861–1865, and they were credited with food production increase that helped the North in winning the war.

When I was growing up the Brown Cornplanter Works produced and sold eight thousand machines a year. He had two hundred men working for him, his shops covering all of a city block except the corner lot he reserved for the new Methodist Church of which he was a regularly attending member.

When we walked the four and a half dusty miles of the Knoxville Road to the County Fair, we passed the old home of Isaac Guliher. Born in Christian

County, Kentucky, he had moved to Sangamon County, Illinois, in 1830, and at seventeen years of age in 1832 had enlisted for the Black Hawk War and served as a private under Captain Abraham Lincoln, moving to Knox County in 1833. In 1858 when Lincoln was on his way from Knoxville to Galesburg to debate with Douglas, he was told this was the house where Isaac Guliher lived and Lincoln got out of his buggy and a mile of buggies and wagons stopped for ten minutes while Lincoln walked in and drank a dipper of cold water with old Sangamon County friends.

Out on the Seminary Street road was the five-hundred-and-forty-seven-acre farm of Daniel Green Burner. He had come to Knox County from New Salem, Illinois, where he had lived four years and had seen young Abraham Lincoln march off to the Black Hawk War. He had traded at the grocery where Lincoln served customers and he had noticed young Lincoln's ways with people. Mr. Burner told a reporter for a Galesburg paper that "Lincoln was as full of fun as a dog is of fleas . . . He would back up against a wall and stretch out his arms; I never saw a man with so great a stretch. He did little things like that to please people . . . He did not go to others for his amusement, but if they wanted fun they came to him and found him full of it . . . ." It would have been nice if I could have worked on Mr. Burner's farm in hay harvest and sat at table and heard him talk about Lincoln and New Salem days.

Knox College, Lombard College, and Brown's Business College gave Galesburg the nickname of "College City." Several times when carrying a two-gallon can of milk I met on streets near Knox College a little man who would nod to me without speaking and to whom I would nod without speaking. He wore a tight-fitting, square-cornered, single-breasted black coat to his knees with buttons running up to his chin. You couldn't see his collar from in front because of his white beard that spread like a fan and covered jaws, chin, and upper lip. Once on Main Street I heard a man say, "That fellow used to know Abe Lincoln." I learned he had been elected Superintendent of Public Instruction of the State of Illinois seven times and served fourteen years, that his room in the State House at Springfield was next to one Lincoln used when a candidate and he and Lincoln had had friendly talks.

This was Newton Bateman, sometimes called "Little Newt," president of Knox College. He said that Lincoln would introduce him as "My little friend, the big schoolmaster of Illinois," and that Lincoln once brought him a letter asking if there should be any corrections in grammar, saying, "I never was very strong on grammar." He saw Lincoln walk back and forth, he said, troubled about the storm that was to sweep the country, saying, "I am nothing but truth is everything." He said too he was the last man to shake hands and say good-bye to President-elect Lincoln before the train pulled out from Springfield bound for Washington.

Newton Bateman was born in New Jersey in 1822. His father, a weaver and a cripple, took his wife and five children West to Illinois in a covered wagon in 1833. Near Jacksonville the Asiatic cholera struck down the mother, and people in a panic fear of the plague saw to it that she was buried in fast time, so fast that the grave wasn't marked. Her youngest son Newton in after years made searches for it but couldn't locate the grave. In his struggle toward an education, he lived for a time on mush and milk at eleven cents a week, walked with a peddler's pack on his back and sold pins, needles, thread, "notions." He had aimed at being a minister, and then changed to teaching. He was principal of the Jacksonville schools and organized the State Teachers Association. He was president of Knox from 1875 to 1892, the longest time any president of Knox had stayed. It was said that under him more graduates went out into the world and made big names for themselves than under any president before him. "He had character," I heard one man say, "and it reached the students."

Little Newt dropped out as president of Knox when he was seventy, went on teaching a few classes while a new president took the chair—John Huston Finley, twenty-nine years old and "the youngest college president in the United States." I met Finley several times, carrying my two-gallon can of milk, but he passed by, his head down, his mind far away. Finley made Knox known over the country as a college where Lincoln and Douglas had debated. He put on an anniversary celebration of the debate on October 7, 1896. I got away from the milk wagon in time to wedge through the crowd for a good look at Chauncey M. Depew in a Prinz Albert coat, with a fedora on his head as he spoke. The day was cold and men on the platform wore overcoats with the collars turned up. I don't remember a word Chauncey Depew said, but I could say I had seen the president of the New York Central Railway and a man who in 1864 made stump speeches over all of New York State for Lincoln for President.

Robert Todd Lincoln, the son of Abraham Lincoln, made a short speech that afternoon. I wondered what kind of talks he had had with his father in the White House, what kind of a Secretary of

War he had been in the cabinets of Presidents Garfield and Arthur. I had read of how at one Republican National Convention after another some delegate always nominated him for President and he would get one vote. In his short speech he didn't say anything I went away thinking about.

In those years as a boy in that prairie town I got education in scraps and pieces of many kinds, not knowing they were part of my education. I met people in Galesburg who were puzzling to me, and later when I read Shakespeare I found those same people were puzzling to him. I met little wonders of many kinds among animals and plants that never lost their wonder for me, and I found later that these same wonders had a deep interest for Emerson, Thoreau, and Walt Whitman. I met superstitions, folktales, and folklore while I was a young spalpeen, "a broth of a boy," long before I read books about them. All had their part, small or large, in the education I got outside of books and schools.

1

Home Folks

Of the house where I was born I remember nothing—a three-room frame house on Third Street, the
second house east of the Chicago, Burlington &
Quincy Railroad tracks, in Galesburg, Illinois. The
date was January 6, 1878, a little after midnight.
The first baby, some three years earlier, was my
sister Mary. They wanted a boy. I was a welcome
man-child.

Mary once pointed to the cradle in later years and said, "When they took me out they put him in." The cradle stood on three legs at each end, and mother told Mary that father had made it. A year and a half later they took me out to put Mart in.

I was born on a cornhusk mattress. Until I was past ten or more years, when we became a family of nine, the mattresses were bedticking filled with cornhusks. As we all slept well on cornhusks and never knew the feel of feather beds till far later years, we were in favor of what we had. Of the slats on which the mattress rested, we sometimes murmured. One would break, then another, till finally the mattress crashed to the floor—and we were suspicious of the new slats.

We moved to another three-room one-story house, on the north side of South Street, three doors west of Pearl. Here I wore dresses and watched my father spade a garden and plant and dig potatoes and carrots. I liked the feel of potatoes and carrots as my fingers brushed the black loam off them and I threw them into baskets. Here we had the mare Dolly— a small bay, old, fat, and slow—kept in a shed at the end of the lot. Dolly pulled us in a four-wheeled, two-seater wagon out from the town streets and houses to where we saw for the first time the open country, rolling prairie and timber, miles of zigzag rail fences, fields of corn and oats, cows, sheep, and horses feeding in pastures. Grazing animals in the open had wonder for me.

We were regular at Swedish Lutheran Church services, though about once a month of a Sunday morning father would throw the harness on old Dolly and the word was, "We are going to the Kranses." Out seven miles near a small coal mine crossroads with a post office named Soperville, on a thirty-acre farm, lived John and his wife Lena Krans. Lena was a cousin of my mother. Those four Swedish-born Americans had warm kinship. Their faces lighted on seeing each other, and their talk ran warm and pleasant. They were all strong for work, liked it, and talked it in those years of their thirties. The Swedish language was hurled back and forth, too swift for us children to be sure what they were saying. But when they talked of the steerage trip from Sweden, six to ten weeks on a sailing ship, their food only the black bread and cheese and baloney they brought along, we knew it was rugged going. Often we heard from father and mother, "In the old country we had *white* bread only at Easter and Christmas. Here in America we have *white* bread every day in the year!"

The Kranses were the nearest kinfolk we had in America except for the Holmes family in Galesburg.

When John and Lena Krans bought their farm in the early 1870s, they worked from daylight to dark eight or nine months of the year till at last the mortgages were paid off. They had help from neighbors in getting in their crops and in turn helped the neighbors. The Kranses became part of the land they owned. Their feet wore paths that didn't change over the years—in the cow pasture with a small creek winding over it, the corn and oat fields, the vegetable garden, the potato patch. John Krans was a landsman, his thoughts never far from his land, the animals, the crops. He could talk about *hästarna*, meaning "horses," so to my mind he seemed part horse.

He was a medium-sized man but he had a loose easy way of carrying his shoulders with his head flung back so he gave the impression of being a big man. His eyes had gleam and his lips had a smile you could see through the beard. Even amid the four walls of a room his head, hair, and beard seemed to be in a high wind. When I sat on his knee and ran my five-year-old hand around in his beard, he called me *min lille gosse* ("my little boy") and there was a ripple of laughter and love in it. He read his Bible and sometimes a newspaper, though most often he liked to read the land and the sky, the ways of horses and corn. He wasn't an arguing man except that with a plow he could argue against stubborn land and with strong hands on leather reins he could argue with runaway horses.

Not often on Sunday did he miss hitching a horse to a light wagon and taking the family to the Lutheran church a mile or two away. I doubt whether he ever listened to a preacher who had less fear and more faith than he had. I have sometimes thought that John Krans pictured God as a Farmer whose chores were endless and inconceivable, that in this world and in worlds beyond God planted and tended and reaped His crops in mysterious ways past human understanding.

The Kranses had a wooden barn with a dirt floor and three horses and four cows that were driven to and from the nearby pasture night and morning. Here we saw hands at udders and milk steaming into pails. The pails were carried up a slope to the house thirty yards away, where the cellar had a clean, hard dirt floor and plank shelves with a long line of crocks into which the milk was poured. We saw the yellow cream at the top of the crocks and once saw cream churned into butter. Here for the first time we drank milk from cows we saw give the milk and ate fried eggs having seen the hens that laid the eggs.

When I was about four we moved two blocks

over to Berrien Street and a ten-room house with a roomy third-story garret running the length of the house and a four-room cellar that had floors in the two front rooms. A two-compartment privy had a henhouse back of it. The lot was three times the size of the South Street place and had a big garden with several gooseberry bushes, a front yard with five tall soft-maple trees, a picket fence, a brick sidewalk, and a ditch in front. It was really two houses and lots. Two sign numbers said we lived at 622 and 624 East Berrien Street. Here the emigrant Swede August Sandburg set himself up, with due humility and constant anxiety, as a landlord. The two east rooms of the first floor, along with the two cellar rooms under them, were rented to different families across the years, never vacant for more than a day or two. And the large upstairs east rooms always had a renter.

My father had never learned to write. His schooling had only taught him to read when his father and mother died in Sweden and he went to work as a chore boy in a distillery. He became a teamster at the distillery and laid by enough money for steerage passage to America. Arriving in New York, Swedes who had kinfolk at Herkimer, New York, sent him to a job in a cheese factory there. After a few months at cheese-making he read a letter from his cousin in Galesburg, Illinois, Magnus Holmes, who wrote that the chances were all good out there. Magnus Holmes had arrived by rail in 1854, the first year the C.B.&Q. reached Galesburg, and joined a gang that built a bridge over the Rock River. He was nineteen. Had he stayed two years longer in Sweden he would have had to serve two years in the Swedish army. His father had spent all his years after he was twenty-one in the Swedish army, till he was retired. And Magnus Holmes had seen army life close up, didn't want to be a soldier, and at nineteen skipped Sweden, took steerage passage for New York on a sailing vessel that buffeted stormy seas for ten weeks and, blown off its course, landed at Quebec.

He reached Albany, took the Erie Canal to Buffalo and railroads to Chicago and Galesburg. There in Galesburg he kept his name of Magnus and changed Holm to Holmes because Holm sounded Swedish and Holmes sounded English. He worked with a railroad construction gang out of Hannibal, Missouri. At a Methodist camp meeting he fell in love with a Swedish girl, a housemaid living with a family that kept slaves. She moved from Hannibal to Galesburg, and Holmes used to call on her when she worked at the Ladies' Dormitory of Lombard College and he had a job in the Q. blacksmith shop forging and hammering bolts. He was interested that she was not merely good-looking and handy as a cook but that she owned a book she was reading, a translation of *Faust*. They were married.

They went to the Knox College campus the afternoon of October 7, 1858, and stood for three hours in a cold northwest wind, in a crowd of twenty thousand, listening to Abraham Lincoln and Stephen Douglas debate. Magnus Holmes voted for Lincoln, but refused to answer Lincoln's call for troops because he hated war and had a conscience about it. So because Holmes hated military service and left Sweden early, to end up at work in a C.B.&Q. Railroad shop, he was there to advise a newcomer cousin to come on West and get a job. The first job my father had was on the Q. railroad with a construction gang at a dollar a day. They lived in bunk cars, cooked their own meals, did their own washing, worked six days a week, ten hours a day.

My mother—young Clara Mathilda Anderson who married my father—told of her mother dying early and her father marrying again. Her mother was a gooseherd in Appuna, and she helped her mother in working with geese and ducks in two ponds on their place. When her stepmother came, "We didn't get along so good. I left Sweden because she was so different from my mother. Letters came from Swedes in America about how things were better there and

I managed to save the money to come over and do my best. There was a chum, like you say, a good friend of mine, came with me and I wasn't lonely."

How my father and mother happened to meet I heard only from my mother. I had asked her how they came to marry and she said: "I was working in a hotel in Bushnell [Illinois], making the beds and helping in the kitchen. He came to Bushnell with the railroad gang. He came to the hotel and saw me and we talked and he said he wanted to marry me. I saw it was my chance and soon went to Galesburg and the Reverend Lindahl married us and we started housekeeping." A smile spread over her face half-bashful and a bright light came to her eyes as she said, "I saw it was my chance." She was saying this years after the wedding and there had been hard work always, tough luck at times, and she had not one regret that she had jumped at her "chance" when she saw it.

My father's hair was straight and black and his eyes, black with a hint of brown, were deep-set in the bone, the skin around them crinkling with his smile or laugh. He was below medium height, weighed about a hundred and forty-eight, was well muscled, and the skin of his chest showed a pale white against the grime when his collar was turned down. No sports interested him, though he did make a genuine sport of work that needed to be done. He was at the

C.B.&Q. blacksmith shop, rated as "a helper," the year round, with no vacations. He left home at six forty-five in the morning, walked to arrive at the Q. shop at seven, and was never late. He mauled away at engine and car parts till twelve, then walked home, ate the noon "dinner," walked back to the shop to begin work at one and go on till the six o'clock whistle, when he stood sledge alongside anvil and walked home.

It would take him ten or fifteen minutes to get the grime off hands, face, and neck before supper. He poured the cistern rainwater from a pail into a tin basin on a washstand, twice throwing the used water into another pail on the floor before the final delicious rinsing at a third basin of the water that had run off the roof into the cistern. The calluses inside his hands were intricate with hollows and fissures. To dig out the black grit from the deep cracks took longer than any part of the washing, and still black lines of smudge failed to come out.

In late spring, summer, and early fall, he would often work in the garden till after dark, more than one night in October picking tomatoes and digging potatoes by the light of a moon. In the colder months he always found something to fix or improve. He liked to sew patches on his jeans pants or his work coat and had his own strong thread and large needle for replacing lost buttons. In those early years he read a weekly paper from Chicago, *Hemlandet,* Swedish for Homeland. Regularly he or mother read aloud, to each other and the children, from the Swedish Bible.

My mother had fair hair, between blond and brown—the color of oat straw just before the sun tans it—eyes light-blue, skin white as fresh linen by candlelight, the mouth for smiling. She had ten smiles for us to one from our father. Her nose was retroussé, not snub. She was five feet five inches high and weighed perhaps one hundred and forty. She had tireless muscles on her bones and was tireless about her housework. She did the cooking, washing, sewing, bedmaking, and housecleaning for her family of nine. At six in the morning she was up to get breakfast for her man and later breakfast for the children. There were meals for all again at noon and at evening. Always there were clothes to be patched, the boys sometimes wearing out a third seat of trousers. As we got into long pants, the knees usually needed patching. Playing marbles in the spring, wrestling, and scuffling, we wore holes at the knees, which went bare till "Mama" patched the holes. That was always our name for her when we spoke to her or of her in the family circle.

My father had respect and affection for Magnus

Holmes, older by fifteen years, and his close friend and adviser. He was well Americanized when August Sandburg arrived at the Holmes house in the early 1870s. He had been in Galesburg more than fifteen years; the men he worked with were mostly Irish and English, and he and Mrs. Holmes learned English so well that they made it the one language spoken in their house. So their four sons never learned to speak Swedish and their daughter Lily learned her Swedish speech by going one summer to the Swedish Lutheran parish school.

From Magnus Holmes, August Sandburg learned many simple and important English words he needed. And this cousin explained where to go and what papers to sign in order to become an American citizen. For years the Holmeses came to the Sandburgs for Thanksgiving dinner and the Sandburgs went to the Holmeses on New Year's Day. Once in our house on Thanksgiving I heard Mr. Holmes talk on the Declaration of Independence and then make clear to my father the Constitution of the United States.

In the Sandburg family the first three children, Mary, Carl August, and Martin Godfrey, learned Swedish fairly well. I am sure that while I was still in dresses, I used only Swedish words to tell what I was wanting. But while the two boys, Emil and Fred, and the two girls, Esther and Martha, who came later knew that *mjölk* was milk, they couldn't count to six in Swedish.

Among the younger church members later there were grumblings and mutterings. "Why must we listen to sermons in Swedish when we can't understand what the preacher is telling us?" After a time there were occasional sermons in English, and changes went on in many churches till all the preaching was in English. This didn't come easy for gray-bearded old-timers who could remember when they sat in their pews two hours with their ears drinking in the beloved syllables of the speech of the homeland that still had its hold over them.

For all that was unjust in living conditions in Sweden that had sent them to America, my father and mother kept a warmth of feeling, a genuine affection, for Swedish people and the language of *gamla hemlandet* (the old country). It stayed deep in their hearts. But they told us little about the Old Country. In their first years in America they had their minds set on making a go of it in the New Country, and perhaps it was a help to forget the Old Country. Then as the years passed they spoke the language of the new land and made many friends and acquaintances who spoke no Swedish, their own later children speaking only English. They became part of the new land.

2

The House on Berrien Street

In the Berrien Street house I was to live growing, formative years from 1882 to 1899, from dresses to short pants to long pants. In that house came babies across ten years, the bright companionable boy Emil, the vague younger one Fred, the beautiful girl Esther and her plain and modest sister Martha.

The ten-room house was a challenge to August Sandburg. He couldn't see himself paying for repairs, and he became carpenter, bricklayer, house painter, paperhanger, cabinetmaker, truck gardener. I was his chore boy, Mart later throwing in. When the roof needed shingling I went up the ladder bringing him shingles. When a cistern had its yearly cleaning, I was let down barelegged to shovel mud and silt into the bucket he drew up with a rope. A chair or table getting wobbly, my father brought it down to his cellar workbench and had me holding a kerosene lamp to light him while he chiseled, fitted, mortised, and hammered. I might after supper have taken my place at the kitchen table to read J. T. Headley's *Napoleon and His Marshals*, from the Seventh Ward school library. And when he called me, I might be saying, "It's a good book and I want to know about Napoleon." But father would say, "Sholly (Charlie), you let Napoleon go for tonight and hold de lamp for me."

Though I had been solemnly christened, with holy water sprinkled on my infant head, by the name of Carl August Sandberg, I decided in the first year or two of school, to use the name Charles. It could have been I had a feeling the name Carl would mean one more Poor Swede Boy while the name Charles had them guessing. Also it was about this time that Mary, Mart, and I decided to write "burg" instead of "berg" in our surname.

Those two letters *ch* bothered many a Swede boy. In our third grade Sheldon's reader was a story titled "Charlie's Chickens," about a boy named Charlie who planted feathers and expected a crop of chickens. One after another, Swede boys Johnson, Nelson, Bostrom, and Hillstrom stood up to read the story aloud. One after another they blurted out "Sharlie's Shickens." The teacher would ask for it again, herself pronouncing it distinctly correct. But from each again came, "Sharlie's Shickens" and the good and patient teacher gave it up. In my seat I laughed inside myself because I had picked the name Charles and had a noble and correct way to fill my mouth with it.

Monday was washday. When I was strong enough, I carried pails of water, from the cistern in the yard, to fill two washtubs. One tub had warm water and a washboard for soaping and rubbing; the other cold water for rinsing, and a wringer attached. On summer and vacation Mondays I often turned the wringer while mother fed the clothes into it. On many winter Mondays I carried the basket of wash out to the backyard clothesline. Often the clothes would get frozen stiff. Coaxing those frozen pieces of cloth to go around the rope clothesline to be fastened with a wooden clothespin was a winter sport with a challenge to your wit and numb fingers in Illinois zero weather, with sometimes a wild northwest wind knocking a shirt stiff as a board against your head. More than once I had to take the basket into the kitchen for the clothes to thaw out while my fingers thawed out.

After the wash was hung, three or four of us would climb on the kitchen table. Mama threw soapy water on the floor and scrubbed and mopped while we played we were on an island or on a housetop floating down a river. After supper or the next morning I would go out and pile the frozen clothes high into the basket and bring them into the house. The noon dinner and the evening supper on Monday, never failing for years, were boiled herring and boiled potatoes, *sill och potatis,* for generations a simple classic menu of which they said with straight faces, "This is what makes the Swedes so strong."

Mama saw to it when we had been too long without a bath. She half filled a washtub with warm water, gave us soap, and told us to scrub. The three sisters would clear out of the kitchen while Mart and I took our washtub bath. Then we would go to bed and the girls would take over.

Mama watched carefully the cellar corner where the cabbage heads were piled in October so that in part of the winter there would be slaw and boiled cabbage. If we forgot, she reminded Mart and me in February of the garden where we could pound, dig, and rassle out one or two bushels of parsnips from the frozen ground.

In the triangle closet under the stairs from the first floor to the cellar Papa used to keep a barrel of apples in winter months, when he could afford it. He put a lock on the door and hid the key. He had seen that when a barrel of apples stood where everyone could get at it, we would soon be at the barrel bottom. He would have put a board over the gap above the door had he known what Mart and I were doing. By hard wriggling our boy bodies could squeeze through the gap and drop down to the apple barrel. We took two apples at a time and only every other day. What we stole wasn't noticed and we said, "When two of us steal two apples and divide them, that's only stealing one apple apiece and stealing one apple isn't really stealing, it's snooking."

Of all our renters I like to think of Joe Elser. He came to our house with a carpenter's tool chest on one shoulder. His belongings had arrived by wagon, and he moved into the two upstairs east rooms, reached by the outside wooden stairway with the coalbin under it.

Joe Elser didn't drink, smoke, or chew tobacco. He didn't go to religious services of any kind. He didn't have any books in his rooms and didn't take any from the Public Library. He never complained, and we never knew him to be sick. He did his own cooking and washing; he darned his socks, mended his clothes, and kept his rooms neat and shipshape.

Joe was tall, strong, spare of build, and we saw him often with his tool chest on his shoulder, carrying it as though he liked it. He was in his early fifties, and his face and hair were grayish, his mustache close-trimmed. He never hurried; in any work he was doing he seemed to have a knack for the next motion after the one now. Joe had fairly regular work as a carpenter across the year. Sometimes because of weather or when a foundation was not finished on a house, he would have days off for sharpening tools and washing bedsheets and pillowcases.

Many a winter night Mart and I went up to see him. He always made us welcome. We began calling him "Uncle Joe" and he enjoyed that. He never referred to his being lonely in any way, and we couldn't believe he had anything sad in his loneliness. We would come up to his kitchen after our supper and he would be setting his table with its oilcloth cover for his supper. He would set chairs for us at the table, then step to the oven and bring out a fresh-baked pie. He would cut the pie and put a quarter of it on my plate and another quarter on Mart's plate. He was proud of the pies he could bake. So were Mart and I. When we told him we had never tasted such good pie, his face had a quiet shine.

Mother said we were going up too often and too early: "You should leave him some pie for himself." And when we came up to see him finished with supper, he would get out a couple of flatirons, hand us a hammer apiece, and bring out a canvas sack of black walnuts, hickory nuts, or hazelnuts. While he joined us in cracking and eating nuts—though we always ate more than he—he did most of the talking.

Joe Elser had been in The War. There was only one war then a man could have been in, the war over the Union and the slaves. Joe had had nearly four years of it. He went in as a private and came out as a private. He had been in battles, and he would take stove wood, put one piece on the floor "where they were lined up" and another "where we stood." Then he would change the wood to show "where they came at us" and "where we counter-charged." He had never been wounded, "but once I had malarial fever bad for six weeks." He didn't make himself out any kind of hero. "You enlisted and then you took what come." The eating was mostly "sowbelly and beans, though sometimes in enemy territory we had rich living on cattle we took and butchered and sometimes there was a sight of pigs and chickens we caught and roasted and fried." They had knapsacks and haversacks at first but threw them away and put everything into a blanket roll. On the march, over the left shoulder went the blanket roll and the right shoulder the rifle—and a cartridge belt around the middle.

This or that was "issued"—uniforms, shoes, socks, rations. You didn't need to buy anything, but if you wanted something special there was the "sutler," who followed the army and set up a store where the army stopped.

When Joe Elser moved away after three or four years we missed him. Out of what he had he made a pretty good life. He had his carpenter's wage of two dollars a day, and thirty dollars a month pension from the government. He liked his work and took pride in being a good carpenter. He was temperate and never talked about temperance. He was lonely and prized his loneliness. Joe Elser never showed any signs of being afraid. He learned somehow to get along without being afraid of what is or of what is to come.

When my father bought the Berrien Street house I am sure he had talked over with his cousin Magnus Holmes the advantages of having enough rooms so you could rent them and have cash coming in every month. Mr. Holmes had bought a used lumberyard office, had it moved on rollers pulled by horses to a vacant lot he owned next to his home, and fixed it over into a house to rent. And when August Sandburg went in for buying a quarter section of land out in Pawnee County, Kansas, he was keeping pace with his cousin, who had bought a quarter section near Holdrege, Nebraska.

Payments he owed on the big house were a load on Papa's mind. So were the payments on that first quarter section of land. He sold this land at some kind of profit and bought another quarter section. I came to know by heart the numbers of the range and the township, because once a year I would write the letter to the County Treasurer of Pawnee County, enclosing a postal money order for the year's taxes. To write that letter Papa would hand me a pencil he prized. Just why he had that pencil, we never knew. The lead was purple and indelible, and Papa called it "indebible." He liked it that you couldn't erase what you wrote.

For several years those one hundred and sixty acres of Kansas farmland haunted the family. Papa talked vaguely about leaving Galesburg and trying his hands on that land way out there. Folders with pictures came from railroads and speculators, showing what bumper crops of wheat and corn, even of pears and apples, could be raised there. "Independent"—we learned that word. The farmer never starves, he can live on what he raises, he is his own boss, he can't be fired from his job, he is "Independent."

Then came the crash, the Panic of 1893 and the Hard Times. We heard how corn went to ten cents a bushel in Kansas. We read of Kansas farmers burning corn for fuel. Kansas land went down in price. What father sold his land for I never heard. But we quit our family discussions about whether a man is more independent working for a railroad or taking his chances as a farmer.

A panic—people running to the banks to find the banks closed, men out of work, charity balls, Coxey's Army in the news for months, men marching on Washington to ask Congress to get them work— and the Hard Times definitely reached Galesburg. Except for watchmen, the railroad shopmen went from a ten-hour to a four-hour day, the checks on payday less than half what they were used to.

We learned to eat bread spread with lard sprinkled with salt, and we liked it. When lard was short we put molasses or sorghum on the bread, which was not so good. We were lucky in our garden giving a bumper crop of potatoes. The land laughed with spuds. As Mart and I helped father dig potatoes and carry the bushel baskets into the cellar, we saw him do the only writing of his we ever witnessed. For each bushel brought in he would chalk on a ceiling rafter a straight vertical line. When there were four verticals he would cross them with a diagonal line, meaning we had five more bushels, by golly.

A little cooperative of neighbors sprang up. They borrowed a horse and wagon and hauled to town a hog from John Krans, "the price near nothing," laughed Krans. Two lots away from us, in front of a small barn in open daylight of a winter day, I first saw a hog killing. The butchering was a drama to us kids. I carried home a bucket of blood from which Mama made a tasty "blood pudding." Mart and I hustled home with a ham and hog sections from which we had across the weeks that winter pork chops, pork loins, side meat, spareribs, cracklings, sowbelly, pig's knuckles, lard for frying and for bread spread.

We learned about "slack" that winter, screenings of coal with no lumps, much cheaper than regular soft coal or bituminous. Into our small heating stove in the kitchen we would shovel it and then keep watch on it, breaking its cinder formations with a poker. If not carefully tended there would be clinkers too large to pass through the grate below. With poker and shovel we would bring up the clinker and put it in its special galvanized iron bucket.

I learned to stoop going through the door to our coalbin under the stairs. I learned to stoop swinging a hammer breaking big lumps into little lumps so they would fit into the coalhod and the stove door. Hands black, nose and ears filled with coal dust, I felt I was earning my board and keep. I would have thought my fate a hard one if I hadn't been reading the *Youth's Companion* with its stories about miners and breaker boys who worked all day and came out with black faces and coal dust in layers. Once I rigged up a small tin can, fastened it to my cap, and went into the dark coalbin playing it was a mine and I had a head lamp like a regular miner.

The kitchen was the only room heated during the cold months. The second-floor bedrooms got what heat went through the door and up the stairs. No heat reached the third-floor garret where Mart and I slept. But we enjoyed, on a below-zero night, standing by the warm kitchen stove, stripping to our underwear and then dashing up two floors and getting under the quilts and snuggling into the cornhusks before Old Mister Zero Fahrenheit could tag us.

The kitchen at first was heated by a stove with lids. At the stove end was a small oblong tank holding water warmed by the hot coals. At first we children called this, as Papa and Mama did, "the rissywarn." When we learned it was a reservoir we went on calling it "rissywarn" out of habit. Later this cookstove went to the cellar, where it served on washdays during the warmer months. Improvements then modern came to the kitchen—a gasoline stove for cooking, and a heating stove with an isinglass door and an ashpan at the bottom. Was it a thousand times or two thousand that I took that ashpan out to the ends of the potato rows to dump one more pan of ashes on the honorable Ashpile?

The kitchen was fifteen feet long and twelve wide, and with cupboard and pantry, sink, gasoline stove and heating stove, a table, eight chairs, and a baby high chair, any passageway was narrow. There we were, a family of, at one time, nine persons in that one room—kitchen, dining room, study room, playroom, workshop. We saw mother mix flour and knead dough, put it in the oven, and bring out brown loaves of bread. We saw coats and trousers patched and socks and stockings darned. We saw father during Hard Times cut leather and peg half-soles on our shoes and cut boy's hair with the family scissors—a ragged-edged haircut but it saved the barber's two bits.

We popped corn and made taffy. We put a flat-iron bottom up on the knees, and with a hammer cracked hazelnuts and walnuts we had picked in October. We made cocked hats out of newspapers. When the lamp needed tending, we went to the cellar for the kerosene can and filled the lamp after trimming the wick. To light the lamp we scratched a blue sulphur match, waited till the blue light was gone and the yellow blaze came, then ran it along the wick and put on the chimney.

We tried a cat once or twice, but it took up too much room and got in the way. Papa was looking on the bright side of things when one day he said Mama could buy a canary and a cage. As it hung high over our heads it didn't get in our way. The canary stayed a year or two but the babies were coming along and each of them was plenty of a pet to look after. In such a room as our kitchen you come to know each other. You learn to mind your own business or there is trouble.

Papa shaved at the kitchen sink before a small looking glass. A serious father with lather over cheeks, chin, and neck looks less serious to his children.

The sound of the scraping razor mowing down the three days' growth of whiskers had a comic wonder for us. He couldn't shave without making faces at himself. There were times that his face took on so fearful and threatening a look we were a little scared.

We saw his razor travel over cheeks, chin, upper lip, below the jaws, everywhere except a limited area under his chin. There he left a small tuft of hair. At intervals over a few weeks we would see him take scissors and trim this goatee. Father didn't mind Mart and me singing the popular song that ended each verse, "With the little bunch of whiskers on his chin."

The pump in the backyard was wooden and stood about fifteen steps from the foot of the stairs going down from the back door. In the warm months water standing in a pail an hour or two didn't taste good and the call was for fresh water, father saying, *"Friskt vatten,* Sholly." I would take an empty galvanized iron pail from the side of the kitchen sink, set the pail under the pump spout, put my two hands on the wooden pump handle, push down, pull up, and go on pumping till water poured out of the spout and filled the pail. Others did this chore at times but I was counted the oldest boy, the handy strong boy who was called on.

In a summer dry spell when the pump handle

came up light and loose, pulling up no water, I knew the water was low and the pump needed "priming." I would go back to the kitchen for a pail of cistern rainwater and pour it down to the leather sucker and the tubing. Then I would push and pull at the pump handle till at last the pump spout was running glad and free saying, "Here is your water!" And on sweltering summer days when butter melted in the kitchen, mother would put it in a small tin pail, tie a doubled grocery string to the handle, and I would let the butter down the well to become cool and hard again.

There were winter mornings when my hands in mittens went round the pump handle and I couldn't budge it. Watching from the kitchen window, they were ready with a pail of hot water. I would skip back to the kitchen for this and pour it down the pump, sometimes running back for a second pail of hot water. After the pump was thawed out I pumped and carried in two pails of water to last the family till the next morning, when again we thawed out the pump. And this meant carrying extra pails of water from the cistern, where there was no pump and you let down your galvanized iron pail and broke the thin ice and pulled the pail up with a rope.

Three or four times when I pushed and pulled at the pump handle no water came. Papa looked it

over, then cut leather and shaped a new sucker. He
let me down into the well on a rope, told me what
to do, and stood looking down telling me more what
to do. I was glad when he pulled me up and we
could say the new sucker worked.

In our early years every house and lot in our block
and the nearby blocks had a fence in front, in back,
and on the sides. The front fences had gates. Slowly
and little by little the fences and gates were taken
away. The frontyard fences went first, then the side
and backyard fences. It began on such streets as
North Broad and North Prairie where the rich and
the well-to-do had their homes. One theory of why
the fences and gates came and vanished goes back
to the early days when people, rich and poor, kept
horses, cows, pigs, and chickens that were always
straying, and if you didn't have your house and yard
fenced they would stray in and forage and trample
your garden. As the roving livestock became fewer,
the North side set the style of tearing fences away
and the rest of the town slowly followed. The year
came when we tore down our frontyard fence and
burned it for kindling wood, saving good boards for
repair jobs. But the side and backyard fences stayed
the seventeen years we lived in that house.

3

A Young Republican

I was six years old on the October night I walked holding my father's hand to Seminary Street near South. It was the first time I saw politics run hot in the blood of men. Hundreds of men were standing in line, two by two. The line ran farther than my eyes could see. Each man had a pole over his shoulder. At the end of the pole swung a lighted torch.

I had never seen one torch in my life, and now of a sudden I saw hundreds of torches in a straight line. Over his shoulders each man had a red, white, and blue oilskin cape. Drippings from the kerosene lamp of the torch fell on the oilskin. My father told me it was "a Republican rally." The sidewalk edges were filled with people waiting to see the march.

We walked north and came to men carrying flambeaus. When the order was given each man blew into a pipe that ran high over his head and they sent up into the air tongues of fire three or four feet high, spreading and weaving like big flowers of fire. I had never seen one flambeau before, and now to see twenty of them blaze up at once was a wonder. When the long red and yellow tongues slowed down and flickered out, the darkness was darker.

We walked farther north to the brass band heading the procession. Leading them as they turned into Main Street was a tall man in yellow pants with a red coat and a red velvet hat nearly as tall as I. He had a stick with a big gold ball on the end and with this stick he motioned the parade how to make the turn. West on Main Street they marched, blowing horns and pounding drums.

On a Main Street corner we watched the parade go by. Every man marching was a Republican. By marching he was showing the Democrats he was a

Republican. My father explained that to me. I heard the marching men holler to people along the sidewalks, and most often it was "Hurrah for Blaine!" or "Blaine for President!" Sometimes a hundred of them would be keeping time with their feet to "Blaine, Blaine, James G. Blaine."

I heard a man on the sidewalk yell, "Hurrah for Cleveland!" Right away came howls from the procession, "And a rope to hang him!" I asked my father about it and he said, "Cleveland is a Democrat. He is against Blaine."

On the way home I asked my father more questions. He gave me the idea that Republicans are good men and Democrats are either bad men, or good men gone wrong, or sort of dumb. And I had a feeling that Cleveland was an ugly man, and if the Republicans got a rope and hanged him I wouldn't be sorry. Nobody had ever explained to me exactly how you hang a man, but if hanging was what the Republicans wanted for Cleveland then I was for it. I was a young Republican, a six-year-old Republican.

A few months later came election. I was told that Grover Cleveland, instead of being hanged, had been elected President. And when Cleveland named a new postmaster for Galesburg it was William Twohig, who lived only two blocks from us in a plain frame house. We called him Billy Twohig. In his backyard he had a sandpile, and when my father had bricklaying to do he sent me with a wheelbarrow over to Billy Twohig's for ten cents' worth of sand. On these trips I came to know him, and I thought he was a pretty good man even though he was a Democrat, even though the ugly Grover Cleveland had named him Galesburg postmaster and boss of all the mail carriers. My father too liked Billy Twohig. I was so mixed up in my head about the Republicans and the Democrats that I didn't ask my father any more questions about it.

I was seven-and-a-half years old when General Ulysses S. Grant died and I went to his funeral. He had died far from Galesburg, I didn't hear where. But Main Street stores closed for the afternoon and the Q. shops and the Brown Cornplanter Works and Frost's foundry shut down too. A parade began at the Q. depot on Seminary Street and moved to Main Street, turned west, and marched to the Public Square. They said it was the longest parade Galesburg had ever seen.

The five long blocks of Main Street sidewalks from Seminary to the Square were crowded with people. It was a hot July afternoon in 1885. My father had been pushed and squeezed and had done some pushing and squeezing himself till at last we stood about three or four feet from the curb in front of the big O. T. Johnson drygoods store. It was good they had made me put on shoes and stockings, because the way I got tramped on would have been worse if I had been barefoot. I tried to see the parade looking between the legs of men ahead of me but all I saw was more legs of more men. I pulled my father's hand and blubbered, "I can't see! I can't see!"

My father lifted me up, stuck his head between my legs, and there I sat straddle of him, and only a giant could see the parade better than I could. There was the marshal at the head of the parade on a skittish sorrel horse with a shiny bridle and with brass buttons, each bigger than a silver dollar, on the saddle. Then came two rows of policemen with nickel-plated stars shining on their blue coats, each with a club hanging from his belt. A fife-and-drum corps followed. The pounding noise they made seemed to shake the buildings and I took a better grip on my father's hat to make sure I wouldn't fall off. Then came a long line of men dressed like they might be going to church on Sunday, marching four in a row.

The Galesburg Marine Band marched past, men walking and blowing into their horns. One man had a big horn that seemed to be wrapped around him and I was puzzled how he got into it. They had on blue coats and blue pants with a stripe down the sides. Their music was slow and sad. It was only twenty years since the war had ended and General Grant was the greatest general in the war and they wanted to show they were sad because he was dead.

Marching past came men wearing dark blue coats and big black hats tied round with a little gold cord having a tassel. They were the G.A.R., the Grand Army of the Republic, and I heard that some of these men had been in the war with General Grant and could tell how he looked on a horse and what made him a great general. Eight or ten of them walked along the sides of a long black box on a black cart pulled by eight black horses. The body of General Grant wasn't in the box, but I could see everybody was even more quiet when this part of the parade passed.

I remember a couple of cannon came past with six or eight horses pulling them. The Negro Silver Cornet Band marched. Their music too was slow and sad. They were the only black faces in the parade, and as they passed I saw faces of men and women light up. I had heard from my father and Mr. Holmes that the war where Grant was the big general was a war for the black people to be free. I didn't quite understand what it was for people to be not free, to be bought and sold like horses. There was nothing like it in Galesburg. But whatever it was it was terrible, and men would shake their heads talking about it. So there was something people liked about seeing the black men playing sad music because General Grant, who had helped them get free, was dead.

A big flag was swinging high over the chunky man carrying it. The end of the pole holding the flag came to some kind of pocket the man had in a belt around his middle. It looked heavy and I could see the sweat rolling on his puffed-out cheeks.

The parade was different from other parades. I had seen a circus parade and people on the sidewalks laughing and hollering at the clowns and elephants and wild animals in cages. I had seen the Republican rally parade with torchlights, and the Democrats on the sidewalks hooted the marching Republicans and the Republicans hooted back. But in this General Grant funeral parade the men marching had straight faces and so did the people on the sidewalks. What boys and girls I saw stood still with straight faces like the old folks. They knew, like I did, it was a day that meant something. Except for the two bands and the fife-and-drum corps and the sound of feet and horse hoofs and wheels on the street stones, you couldn't hear much of anything.

Even the slow sad music seemed quiet. I think the only smile I saw while the parade was passing was once when my father turned his face up toward me and felt good over the way he had fixed it so I could see the parade.

I remember how hard I tried to think about what the war was and what General Grant did that made him the greatest general of all. And I heard he had been President. I heard too he was one of the high men of the Republican party and the Republicans would miss him, and that some Democrats who had been in the war with him liked the way he did things and the way he treated them and these Democrats were sorry along with the Republicans.

The parade over, my father let me down. We walked along Main Street among thousands of people, and then home. I could see it was a day that meant something to my father. In some store windows I noticed pictures of General Grant with black cloth hung around them. I couldn't see that he looked so different from other men with whiskers over the whole face and the hairs cut close. He didn't look much different from Mr. Grubb, the Lombard professor who lived across the street from us and milked his Jersey cow each morning before starting out for his classes. And then I said to myself that even though Professor Grubb's face was nearly exactly like General Grant's face, if he should die there wouldn't be any parade as we had seen for General Grant. I went to bed that night saying I hoped sometime I would know more about the war, about the black people made free, about Grant the general and what it was like to be President and the head man of the government in Washington.

4

Hungry to Learn

One of my most vivid early memories is our first
home Bible, a small Swedish-language Bible. I was
about four years old, and it was in the Berrien Street
house, in the second-floor bedroom of my father and
mother. It was winter, with winds howling outside.
Mary and I heard father read a chapter by the light
of a small kerosene lamp. Several times that week
I went to where the Book lay on top of a bureau,

and I opened it and turned the pages. I asked my mother to point out certain words I remembered. I took comfort in mother saying it would be clear to me when I started school and learned to read.

The day came when I started off for the Fourth Ward school, four blocks from our house. But the next year our block on Berrien Street was moved over into the Seventh Ward and we had to walk six blocks more to school. The secrets of the alphabet were unlocked for me. We recited in class and we learned that every word has a right way to say it and a wrong way. It came clear that any language is a lot of words and if you know the words you know the language.

One winter Friday afternoon when I was in the fifth grade I took home the first volume of John S. C. Abbot's *The History of Napoleon Bonaparte* and most of Saturday and Sunday I sat in an overcoat at the north window of our third-floor garret and read the book. The next week I did the same with the second volume. I had heard about Napoleon so often I wanted to see what kind of fighter he was. I got a picture in my mind of what Napoleon was like and I buckled a leather strap around my middle, ran where the strap would hold it a sword I whittled from a lath, and walked from garret to cellar and back giving orders to my marshals like Napoleon.

In the sixth grade Miss Goldquist kept at us about getting "the reading habit," saying, "You don't know what good friends books can be till you try them, till you try many of them." One of her favorite words was "ed-u-ca-tion," and she said you could never get enough of it. I read a row of history books by Jacob Abbott and John S. C. Abbot, J. T. Headley's *Napoleon and His Marshals* and *Washington and His Generals*. I found Thomas W. Knox's *Boy Travellers* in different countries a little dry and not up to Hezekiah Butterworth's *Zigzag Journeys* over the world. What time I could steal from lessons I turned the pages of Champlin's *Young Folks' Cyclopaedia of Persons and Places*, and *Young Folks' Cyclopaedia of Common Things* from the school library.

Best of all was the American history series by Charles Carleton Coffin. *The Boys of '76* made me feel I could have been a boy in the days of George Washington and watched him on a horse, a good rider sitting easy and straight, at the head of a line of ragged soldiers with shotguns. I could see Paul Revere on a horse riding wild and stopping at farmhouses to holler the British were coming. I could see old curly-headed Israel Putnam, the Connecticut farmer, as the book told it: "Let 'em have it!" shouted Old Put, and we sent a lot of redskins head over heels into the lake . . . A few days later . . . the

French and Indians ambushed us. We sprung behind trees and fought like tigers. Putnam shot four Indians . . . one of the Frenchmen seized Roger's gun, and the other was about to stab him, when Put up with his gun and split the fellow's head open."

I met General Nathanael Greene and watched him fight and in the nick of time draw off his soldiers and then come back when the time was right to win. He was a whiz at retreating and then, when the enemy didn't expect him, making a comeback and crippling the enemy or breaking him. I read about Lord North, the British Head Minister who ran the war. I saw a picture of the fathead and agreed with another boy, "I could cut the guts out of him."

The Boys of '76 had me going through the book just for the pictures. Whoever drew them was as good for the book as the author, but all it said on the title page was ILLUSTRATED.

I was thankful to Mr. Coffin for other books like *Old Times in the Colonies*. You were right there with those people building huts and cabins, clearing timbers, putting wooden plows to new land and plowing around the stumps while keeping an eye on the shotguns ready for the Indians. In *The Story of Liberty* he tried to tell what went on over in Europe that sent people heading across the ocean to America. You learned about "tyrants" and "tyranny" and people slaughtered in fights and wars about religion.

When I took home Mr. Coffin's *The Boys of '61* and two or three more on the Civil War I found they were dry compared with *The Boys of '76* and his earlier books. I couldn't understand this because I read that Mr. Coffin had been a war correspondent in the Civil War, went with the armies and was on the spot when some of the hottest battles were fought. When he wrote about a war he had seen, it wasn't worth reading. I puzzled over this: "It was a bigger war in '61 than '76 and maybe so big he couldn't get his head around it. Or maybe following the armies he got sick of the war, so disgusted that when he started writing about it he tried to hide his disgust but it got into his book without his knowing it."

Every boy except the dumbest read those two books by James Otis, *Toby Tyler; or, Ten Weeks with a Circus* and *Tim and Tip; or, The Adventures of a Boy and a Dog.* The library copies were ragged, dog-eared, thumb-and-finger dirtied, and here and there a pencil had written, "Good" or "Gee whiz."

The detective story books of those school days were mostly Old Cap Collier at a nickel apiece. We read them in the schoolroom behind a geography, and traded with each other. But soon I went back to Champlin's *Young Folks' Cyclopaedia of Persons and Places.* Later came Nick Carter and his sidekick

Chick, keener than Old Cap Collier. The year came, though, when I decided that detective stories were mostly tricks.

We read *Huckleberry Finn* and *Tom Sawyer* by Mark Twain but they didn't get the hold on us that other books did. They seemed to be for a later time. It was the same with the novels of Charles Dickens.

We had a first book in physiology in school and then one or two more. We read about alcohol and saw what happens to a drunkard's stomach. But I wasn't worried about my father's stomach because never did he go into any of the town's dozen saloons. When on a cold winter night Papa took down his pint bottle of pure grain alcohol and poured a spoon or two into a cup of black coffee, we knew the bottle would be finished that winter and there wouldn't be another till the next winter. The Kranses, the Holmeses, and the Swedish Lutherans we knew kept away from beer, wine, and whisky if only for the money it wasted that they could spend for things they liked better.

There came the day I entered a declamation contest to speak a piece against the evils of alcohol. On Seminary two blocks south of Berrien Street an afternoon Sunday school named the Mission drew boys and girls, about a hundred, from Berrien and other streets. The frame building, painted brown but with the paint peeling away, stood across the street from the Q. machine shop, next to the Peoria branch of the Q. The meetings ran through the fall and winter, and the teachers were mostly students from Knox College. We had good times at the Mission. As a member of the Mission's Junior Epworth League, I was once a delegate to a convention in Monmouth, sixteen miles from Galesburg, the farthest I had ever been away from home. And we put on "entertainments." After rehearsing a program three or four times, we gave it of an evening for grownups and children. I sang once in a quartet and once I took the part of a tramp in a one-act play.

But it was the Demorest Silver Medal Declamation Contest that had all of us at the Mission buzzing. Mr. Demorest, a rich man in the East who had made his money getting out a magazine giving women ideas and patterns for dresses, was "a total-abstinence man." He never drank a drop of liquor himself and he wanted to see every saloon in America put out of business. So he had thought up the Demorest medal contests in which the young people of any school or neighborhood would speak pieces against alcohol. Mr. Demorest sent us each a book to pick out the piece to speak in the contest. I picked the shortest piece in the book, and the last line was: "The world moves!" I practiced many ways to say it and couldn't decide whether to give it slow and drawn out or fierce and fast like a shot in the dark.

It was all very exciting, because whoever won the silver medal in our contest would go into another contest with other silver-medal winners. Then whoever won that contest would get a gold medal. Then the gold-medal winners would go into a contest for a diamond medal. We talked about it and agreed that if any of us won a diamond medal that would be high enough and we would be satisfied.

The night of the contest came and there was the biggest crowd the Mission had ever seen. There we sat, a row of us on the platform looking at the audience and the audience looking at us. We picked out faces from them and they picked out faces from us. They smiled and we tried not to smile. When there is a silver medal hanging over you, you don't smile, or anyhow we thought you're not expected to.

Four boys and four girls stood up one by one and gave their declamations. About the middle of the program my name was called. I walked to the center of the platform feeling good that what I had to remember was only half as long as some of the others. I blurted out my opening sentences wondering how it sounded to the people out there. Near the middle of my declamation I had to stop. I didn't know what was coming next. I reached up and around and somehow my mind pulled down what I wanted and I went on to the end and gave "The world moves!" fierce and fast like a shot in the dark and saw more faces laughing than sober.

The judges didn't make us wait long to hear who was the winner. I knew I had done a little worse than any of the others on the program, and I didn't expect to be excited or proud about whoever got the prize. But when one of the judges stood up and told us who was the winner, there I was, excited and proud. The judge was saying, "It gives us great pleasure to announce that the winner of the Demorest Silver Medal is Miss Mary Sandburg."

A book we owned each year till it got lost was *Hostetter's Illustrated United States Almanac,* given away every New Year's Day. Half the almanac was filled with good words for Hostetter's Stomach Bitters. There was advice too on how to get rid of warts, corns, boils, how to get a ring off a swollen finger, what to do about a rusty nail in the foot and other ailments. Five pages had funny drawings with jokes under them. We read Hostetter's out loud in the kitchen and talked over the points of the jokes and what the "wise sayings" meant.

We didn't know we were getting education while having fun, Mary, Mart, and I, in that crowded kitchen when we read *Hostetter's Almanac* to each other. It was crammed with all sorts of facts new to us and interesting—the morning and evening stars for any month in the year, the ocean tides, the velocity of the earth, eclipses, and so on. We were hungry to learn.

The first biography I owned was of a size I could put in one of my vest pockets. I was going along to the Seventh Ward school when I found it on a sidewalk. It had been rained on and I brushed the dirt off and smoothed it where the top corner had been scorched. When I measured it later it was two and three-fourths inches long and one and one-half inches wide. The front cover had gloss paper and a color picture of the head and shoulders of a two-star general in a Confederate gray uniform. The title read *A Short History of General P. T. Beauregard.*

There were thirteen pages of reading in fine print. Inside the back cover was a list of a "Series of Small Books," histories of Civil War generals, fifty of them, with a notice of "other series in preparation." And here you learned how to get these books. It said "Packed in Duke's Cigarettes."

I couldn't think of buying ten-cent packages of Duke's Cameo or Duke's Cross-Cut cigarettes for the sake of filling my vest pockets with histories, nice as they were. Cigarettes had a bad name among us kids; we believed only "dudes" and "softies" smoked them. Our physiology books had warned us that tobacco had nicotine in it and nicotine is a poison. And with cigarettes you were supposed to inhale and take the poison straight into your lungs. This could lead you into consumption, or anyhow it would weaken your wind and slow you down as a runner or ballplayer. When we bought Virginia Cheroots at five for a nickel or the ten little "cigaroos" for a nickel and smoked them, we were like strong men ready to take a chance on what real tobacco could do to us.

I scouted around and found three men who smoked Duke's Cigarettes "once in a while for a change." One of them was saving the books for himself. The other two saved them for me. After a while I had the histories of Beauregard, Cornelius Vanderbilt, and Sarah Bernhardt, *The Life of T. De Witt Talmage*, and the lives of George Peabody, James B. Eads, Horace B. Claflin, and Robert Ingersoll. They changed from *History of* to *Life of*.

In the list I noticed John Ericsson, the inventor of the *Monitor*, the Swede who helped the North win the war. I tried but couldn't scare up a copy of the Ericsson. A Swede boy pulled one out of his vest pocket one day and grinned at me. He knew I wanted it. I offered him a penny for it and went as high as a nickel and he shook his head. Then he let me borrow it and I let him borrow my Sarah Bernhardt. He had heard she kept a coffin in her bedroom and liked to stretch out in it to rest. I showed him where the book told about that. "Gee!" said the Swede boy, "I sure want to read that book." I offered to trade him the Sarah Bernhardt for his John Ericsson. He said maybe and next day told me he had talked it over with his Swede father and mother and they said, "No, you keep the John Ericsson."

So there was my vest-pocket library of biography and history. There were days I carried the eight books, four in the upper right-hand vest pocket and four in the upper left. I had books I didn't have to take back to the Seventh Ward school or the Public Library. I was a bookowner.

One Monday morning, a bright summer day, mother was doing a wash in the cellar. I came in to see a well-dressed man talking to her. She had quit washing and was listening to him. He was showing her a sample of a book. Here were the covers and here were sample pages—the real book was five times bigger. Mama's face and eyes were shining. He was saying that education is important. And how do you get education? Through books, the right kind of books. Now you have this *Cyclopedia of Important*

Facts of the World around and the children can't help reading it. Knowledge—that is what counts when your children go out in the world—knowledge! "The more they learn the more they earn!"

Mother was a little dazed by now. He was speaking her own mind as to education and knowledge. Papa would have been scowling and shaking his head. Mother was more than interested. She took the sample and turned pages. She looked down into my face. Would I like the book? I said yes in several ways. She signed her name and she had the required seventy-five cents ten days later when the man came with the book.

About this *Cyclopedia* father grumbled—a waste of money, let the children get "eddication" in the schools. It was later he made a real fuss. This time I was there again when the book agent came, not the same man, but well dressed and polite, handy with his tongue, like the first one. His book was three times bigger than the *Cyclopedia*, bigger pages, two columns to the page, many pictures, *A History of the World and Its Great Events*, with special attention to the famous battles of all time. Mother was not quite so bright, not so sure, as the last time. But I was surer I would like this book. Mother signed again. This time it was a dollar and a half, more than a day's pay of my father. But mother had the money when the book came two weeks later.

I won't go into the scene father made when he saw the book and heard the price. We were heading for the Knoxville poorhouse. If it ever happened again he didn't know what he would do. It ended mother's listening to book agents.

Mother had visions and hopes. She could say with a lighted face, "We will hope for the best," as I bent my head over *A History of the World and Its Great Events*. Father would stand over me saying, "Wat good iss dat book, Sholly?" And I had no answer. I didn't like his saying such a thing, but I had some dim realization too that he had in mind mortgages on which payments must be made.

When I finished the Seventh Ward school, I could feel I was growing up, halfway toward being a man. It was a change to walk a mile twice a day to the Grammar School downtown and home again. They came from all ends of town to the Grammar School, many new faces to see, many more boys and girls from the well-off families.

The Grammar School stood a short block from the Public Square. Between stood the Old First Church, built more than forty years before by the First Settlers. Straight across the street from the Grammar School stood the two-story house of Henry R. Sanderson. He had a long white beard and a quiet face and had been mayor of Galesburg when Lincoln came to debate with Douglas in 1858. We heard he had taken Abraham Lincoln into his house as a guest and had helped with towels and warm water for Lincoln to take a bath.

In the eighth grade I had Miss Frances (Fanny) Hague, truly a great teacher. She knew books and would have loved them whether she taught them or not. She had traveled Europe and could make cities and ruins there come alive for us. The high spot for me under her teaching was *A Brief History of the United States;* the title page didn't tell who wrote it. It was for me the first book that tried to tell the story of our country from the time of the early Indians through Grant as President. It was stuffy and high-falutin in style, yet it made me see the American Story in new lights. Miss Hague knew history too and often gave color and good sense to passages in it.

When I left Miss Hague's room my mind kept going back to it. I wasn't sure what education was but I was sure that I got a little under her teaching. From then on until several years later, what schooling I got was outside of schools, from reading books, newspapers, and magazines, from watching and listening to many kinds of people and what they were doing and saying.

5

Days of Play and Sport

On the wooden sidewalks of Berrien Street we played
one kind of mumble-peg and in the grass of the front
yard or the grass between sidewalk and gutter ditch
we played the more complicated and interesting kind
with jump-the-fence, thread-the-needle, plow-forty-
acres, and plow-eighty-acres. On the wooden sidewalks we spun tops, flipped jackstones, chalked tit-
tat-toe. On the street we played baseball, two-old-

cat, choose-up, knocking-up-flies. In shinny any
kind of club would do for knocking a tin can or a
block of wood toward a goal, though the fellow with
a plow handle had the best of it. And duck-on-a-
rock had its points—knocking a small rock off a
large rock and then running to pick up your own
rock to get back to taw without being tagged.

After we had seen the commencement Field Day
on the Knox or Lombard campus, we put on our own
field day, barefoot in the summer dust of Berrien
Street. Some boy usually had a two-dollar-and-a-
half Waterbury watch and timed us as we ran fifty
yards, one hundred yards, a few seconds slower than
the college runners, and five or six seconds under
the world's record. We knew how near we came to
the college records in the standing broad jump, the
running broad jump, the hop-skip-and-a-step, the
standing high jump and the running high jump.
Whoever could throw a crowbar the farthest was
counted put-and-shot "champeen." We did everything the college athletes did except the pole vault.
The mile run we did afternoons, breaking no records
except some of our own, yet satisfying ourselves that
there is such a thing as "second wind" and if you
can get it you can finish your mile.

Straight across the street from the house next
east to ours was an average two-story frame house,

with a porch. In the street in front of this house was our home base when playing ball. Often we saw on that porch in a rocking chair a little old woman, her hair snow-white with the years. She had a past, a rather bright though not dazzling past. She could lay claim to fame, if she chose. Millions of children reading the McGuffey and other school readers had met her name and memorized lines she had written. For there was in the course of her years no short poem in the English language more widely published, known, and recited than her lines about "Little Things":

> Little drops of water,
>   Little grains of sand,
> Make the mighty ocean
>   And the pleasant land . . .
> Little deeds of kindness,
>   Little words of love,
> Help to make earth happy
>   Like the heaven above.

She was Julia Carney. Her sons Fletcher and James were Universalists and Lombard graduates, Fletcher serving three or four terms as mayor of Galesburg. There she sat in the quiet of her backward-gazing thoughts, sometimes gently rocking, an image of silence and rest, while the air rang with boy screams, "Hit it bang on the nose now!" "Aw, he couldn't hit a balloon!" "Down went McGinty to the bottom of the sea!" Rarely she turned her head to see what we were doing. To us she was just one more nice old woman who wouldn't bother boys at play. We should have heard about her in school. We should have read little pieces about her in the papers. She has a tiny quaint niche in the history of American literature under which one line could be written: "She loved children and wrote poems she hoped children would love."

In early years we would stop our play and follow the lamplighter when he came along before dusk. He carried a small ladder he would set against the lamp-post, and we would watch him climb up, swing open the door of the glass case holding a gas burner, turn on the gas, and with a lighted taper put the flame to the escaping gas. Then he would climb down and move on from the corner of Pearl and Berrien to the corner of Day and Berrien, a block east. Then came the electric lights, one arc lamp at every second corner, exactly in the center of the four street crossings, high enough so a man driving a load of hay couldn't reach up and touch the globe. The lamplighter was gone. We missed him.

It wasn't long before the fathers and mothers along Berrien Street had new troubles with their boys. Under that electric light at Day and Berrien the boys had a new playground. They could turn night into day. There was night baseball, night shinny, night duck-on-a-rock, night tug-of-war. There were winners yelling because they had won. There were losers yelling that next time they would make the winners eat dirt. Vehement remarks floated through windows into rooms where honest Q. shopmen and worthy railroad firemen and brakemen were trying for a little sleep.

One of the sleepers who couldn't sleep had a voice like a big-league umpire when one night he clamored from his bedroom window, "You boys shut up and go home with you. If you don't I'll get the police on you." The noise stopped. We sat cross-legged on a patch of grass next to a sidewalk and talked in whispers: "Do you s'pose he means it?" "Aw, we got a right to holler, this is a free country." "Yeah, but what if he means it? We'll get run in." "Yeah, I don't want no patrolwagon ride." About then came a woman who wanted her sonny-boy; she took him by one ear and led him away and his face had a sheepish look. Then came two men, fathers. They spotted their boys, collared them, and led them away like two sheep for slaughter. Mart and I went home. If we didn't get into the house by nine o'clock we would get scoldings or worse.

On a later night the boys forgot themselves and the hullabaloo they made could be heard a block away. Then as promised, the patrol wagon came. Before it could stop, five or six boys skedaddled. That left five or six of us who weren't going to run and show we were scared. We stood in a huddle waiting. Out of the patrol wagon came two policemen, their nickel-plated stars shining on their coats. One of them, Frank Peterson, weighed about two hundred and twenty pounds, and looked like a battleship coming toward us. We expected hard words from Policeman Peterson. But he spoke in a soft voice like what he was saying was confidential. "Don't you boys know you're disturbing people who are trying to sleep?" What could we say to a quiet intelligent question like that? One boy said, "Yes," another, "Well, you know we were just trying to have some fun." "Yes," said Peterson, again quiet and confidential-like, "but ain't there some way you can have your fun without keeping people awake that's trying to sleep?" We had come to like Policeman Peterson. We saw he wasn't mad at us and it didn't look like we were going to be put in the wagon and hauled to the calaboose. We said yes, we would try to have our fun without making so much noise.

Before walking away Peterson said, "Now that's a promise, boys, and I expect you to keep it. If you don't stop your noise, we'll have to run you in." And his voice got a little hard as he said, "Remember that. We don't like to arrest young fellows like you but sometimes we have to do it." That word "arrest" stuck in our ears. They could have arrested us. When you're arrested that means you're a criminal. And if you're a criminal, where are you?

The patrol wagon drove away. When the rumble of its wheels had died away we sat on the grass and talked in low tones near a whisper. All of us agreed that from now on we had better try to have our fun without yelling. All agreed except the boy who had on another night said, "Aw, we got a right to holler, this is a free country." This boy guessed he'd rather stay away and have some other kind of fun than come around and be a nice boy like the police told him. And he did stay away and later he took to the poolrooms and the saloons and still later put in a year in the Pontiac reformatory for petty larceny.

We went on playing under the electric light and trying to keep quiet but it was a strain. I had a job where I had to report at six-thirty in the morning and had gone home early one night, leaving the boys in a hot game of shinny, back in their old hooting and yelling. They told me next day that a railroad fireman had come out in his nightshirt with a club and a revolver. He shot in the air twice to show the gun was loaded. He sent a bullet into a sidewalk plank and had them look at the bullet. He was wild-eyed, cursed them, slapped one of them, kicked another, then took out a watch and said if every last one of them wasn't gone in two minutes he would shoot to kill. Half the boys ran and the rest went away on a fast walk. From then on not as many boys came to that corner at night; it became reasonably quiet, and decent people could sleep. There was hate for the shooting-iron fireman. And Policeman Frank Peterson we would point out with, "He ain't a bad fellow, do you know?"

Four lots to the east of our house was a vacant double lot where later we laid out a small diamond. At the time a good-natured Jersey cow was pastured there. We never hit the cow but when the ball landed near her and the fielder ran toward her it disturbed her. Also it disturbed the owner of the cow, who said he would have the police on us. So we played in the street till the day the cow was gone and we heard it had been sold. Then we went back to our pasture.

On the narrow lot next to the pasture was Mrs. Moore's house. She was the widow of a Civil War veteran, living alone on a federal pension. She was a tall woman with dark hair streaked with gray—a quiet woman, smoking her clay pipe, keeping to herself and raising vegetables and flowers. She had the nicest all-round flower garden in our block, the front of her lot filled with hollyhocks, begonias, salvia, asters, and morning glories climbing the fences. First base was only ten feet from her fence and every so often a fly or a foul ball would go over into her potatoes, carrots, and hollyhocks. A boy would climb the fence and go stomping around hunting the lost ball. At such times as Mrs. Moore stood between the boy and the place where he believed the ball fell it was not pleasant for either party concerned. "Why must you boys do this to my place?" she would ask. When the boy answered, "We'll try never to do it again," her reply would come, "See that you don't do it again. I don't want to make trouble for you boys."

Again and again we sent the ball over into her well-kept yard. She tried scolding but she just naturally wasn't a scold. She quietly hinted she might have to go to the police, but she didn't go to the police or to our parents. She had property rights and we were trespassing on her property, and she forgave us our trespasses even though we went on trespassing. She was a woman of rare inner grace who had gathered wisdom from potatoes and hollyhocks.

In our early games played in the street, the bat was a broom handle, the ball handmade—a five-cent rubber ball wrapped round with grocery string. The home plate was a brick, first base a brick, second base a tin can, third another tin can. We played barehanded till we learned how to stuff a large man-sized glove with cotton, wool, or hair to take the sting out of a fastball.

The days came when we played in the cow pasture with a Spalding big-league regulation ball. We gathered round the boy who first brought it. "Well, what do you know!" we said, "a dollar and a half." And we told it around as a kind of wonder, "We been playing today with a dollar and a half"—the same ball that Amos Rusie was throwing in the big league, the same ball Big Bill Lange was hitting with the Chicago team. When I carried Chicago newspapers and read sports news I learned about the "elusive pill" thrown by Amos Rusie. I was among those who grieved later to hear of Amos Rusie taking to drink, being dropped from major and minor clubs, and being found one day digging gas mains at a dollar-fifty a day. He was doing ten cents a day better than my father at the Q. shop but still I was more sorry for him than for my father.

When Galesburg played Chillicothe or Peoria or Rock Island on the Knox campus, the Berrien Street kids, lacking the two bits' admission, watched the games through knotholes in the fence. Or we climbed a tree fifty yards from the home plate, found a crotch to sit in, and had as much fun as though we were in the two-bit bleachers.

The most exciting baseball year the town had was when a City League was organized and played one or two games a week. The Main Street clerks had one team, the railroad shopmen another, and there were two other teams. Out of the tall grass around Victoria came a team that had surprises. Galesburg had picked the best nine in the town to meet them and the word was that maybe Galesburg would "goose-egg" them. But the country boys played fastball, among them the Spratt brothers, Bob and Jack, who later went into minor-league clubs. Their center fielder was a tall gawk wearing a derby! As the game got going Victoria took the lead by one or two runs and kept the lead till near the closing inning, when Galesburg with one out got two men on bases and one of its heaviest sluggers came to bat. He hit the ball high and handsome and sent it sailing away out to deep center field. The tall gawk in the derby made a fast run, made a leap for it, caught it with one hand and threw it straight to second to catch a man off base—and Victoria was victorious in one of the craziest, sweetest pieces of baseball drama I have ever seen.

On many a summer day I played baseball starting at eight in the morning, running home at noon for a quick meal and again with fielding and batting till it was too dark to see the ball. There were times my head seemed empty of everything but baseball names and figures. I could name the leading teams and the tailenders in the National League and the American Association. I could name the players who led in batting and fielding and the pitchers who had won the most games. And I had my opinions about who was better than anybody else in the national game.

An idea began growing in me that if I played and practiced a lot I might become good enough to get on a team. Once on a minor league team I would have my chance to show what I could do and I might end up in the majors—who knows about a thing like that? It was a secret ambition. In what spare time I could find I played with the boys and did fairly well in left field on a scrub team.

Then came an afternoon in early October when I was sixteen. I had managed to buy secondhand a fielder's glove, a regular big-league affair I was proud of. Skinny Seeley and I went to a pasture and knocked up flies. He hit a high one to me and I was running top speed for it. I believed I would make a brilliant catch, the kind I would make when maybe one of the minor league clubs had taken me on. Suddenly my right foot stashed into a hole and I fell on my face. When I looked at my foot I saw a gash in the shoe leather and blood oozing from the tangled yarn of the sock. In the hole there was a broken beer bottle, and into this my foot had crashed.

I limped across the pasture, about a block, to the house of Dr. Taggart. Out on his front porch he had me take off the shoe, then slowly the sock. He cleaned the cut, picked out yarn and glass, applied antiseptic. Then he brought out a curved needle and sewed four stitches at about the middle of the foot just below the instep. He bandaged my foot and I limped home. My mother spoke sorrow and pity. My father asked when would I ever learn any sense and quit wasting my time with baseball.

From that day on I was completely through with any and all hopes of becoming a big-time ballplayer. I went on playing occasional games, but those four stitches marked the end of my first real secret ambition.

6

Fair and Circus Days

We were between nine and twelve when we took in the Knox County Fair one year after another for three years. We walked the four and a half miles to the fairgrounds just outside of Knoxville—Husky Larson, his brother Al, and one or two other boys. The dust lay thick on the road. We walked barefoot, carrying our shoes and putting them on when we came to the fairgrounds so we wouldn't get our bare toes stepped on in the crowds. We walked to save the round-trip railroad fare and after paying twenty-five cents admission, we watched our few nickels.

One nickel went to the man who had the new and amazing Edison Talking Phonograph. Around the machine stood people watching what it did to the faces of those who clapped on the earphones and were listening. Some faces sober and doubting stayed sober and came away saying, "It works, dog-gone it, you can hear that brass band playing like it was right here on the fairgrounds." Most faces, however, wore smiles, and came away saying, "It's pretty cute, I tell you. The machine talks like it's human."

We stepped up with our nickels. We plugged our ears with the phone ends. We watched the cylinder on the machine turning. We heard a voice saying this was the Edison Talking Phonograph and that next we would hear a famous brass band playing. We looked at one another and nodded and smiled, "It works! I can hear it! Ain't it the dog-gonedest thingamajig? I wouldn't believe it if I wasn't hearing it."

We watched the stallions and mares, bulls and cows, boars and sows, cocks and hens—and the judges awarding prizes and blue ribbons. We saw farmers proud of what they had bred and raised. We felt something in the air very different from a circus. Many a farmer and his boy had come to learn. Their work the year round was in trying to make the land and the animals bring bigger crops and more food. They had on their best clothes but their muscles stood out in little humps and bunches so that their coats hung on them. Their women carried the signs of hard work, some of them taking pride in the jellies and preserves they had entered for showing. The biggest Knox County potato of the year was worth seeing, as also the largest rutabaga.

We didn't have the two bits for grandstand seats to see the horse races. We stood at the board fence next to the grandstand and watched the fastest horses in Knox County—saddle horses, thoroughbreds, pacers and trotters, with drivers in sulkies with high wheels, spokes of wood, and the rims iron. Several of the drivers, like Fred Seacord, we had seen on the streets of Galesburg exercising their horses and getting them used to the sulkies.

There was a "special feature"—"The Only Pacing Dog in the World." Occasionally we had seen Mr. Redfield with his Irish setter on Main Street. And we knew it was no common dog. Now at last we saw Mr. Redfield come out on the track with his horse and sulky. Alongside the right wheel so the grandstand could see him was the Irish setter, handsome with his coat of brown hair gleaming, his gait that of a pacer, the legs in that peculiar continuous sidewise throw. Twice around the half-mile track went the pacing dog. He wasn't as fast as pacing horses but the crowd believed he was the only pacing dog in the world and they cheered him and Mr. Redfield.

That year we caught a ride in a hayrack from the fairgrounds to Galesburg. Arriving home we talked most about having heard the first Edison Talking Phonograph in Knox County and having seen the only pacing dog in the world. About the dog Papa merely remarked that it was interesting. That Edison Talking Phonograph, however, giving you a band concert without bringing you the band, that was curious and he said, "Wat will dey tink up next?" When the talking machine later came to a vacant store on Main Street he spent several nickels listening to the newfangled contraption.

When the circus came to town we managed to shake out of sleep at four o'clock in the morning, grab a slice of bread and butter, and make a fast walk to the Q. yards to watch the unloading in early daylight. A grand clear voice the man had who rode his horse a half-block ahead of the elephants in the parade and cried out, "The elephants are coming, watch your horses!" First to one side of the street and then the other he cried it and those who had skittish horses watched them.

The great P. T. Barnum himself never met my eyes but on a bright summer morning I did see Mr. Bailey of the firm of Barnum & Bailey in a black swallowtail coat giving orders and running the circus in the big green pasture that soon was subdivided into city lots. And with the other kids who had seen Bailey I joined in saying, "Wasn't he something to look at? And think of it, he's nearly as great a man as Barnum himself!"

After the unloading we went home for a quick breakfast and then a run to the circus grounds, a big pasture at Main and Farnham near the city limits. If we were lucky we got jobs at carrying water for the elephants or lugging to the big tent the boards for the audience to sit on. After three or four hours of this work we were presented with slips of paper that let us in to see the big show in the afternoon. If we hadn't been lucky and if we didn't have the fifty cents for a ticket we tried to slide under the canvas and crawl to where we could peek through boards and between legs to see the grand march, the acrobats, the trapezists, the clowns, the hippodrome chariot race given before our eyes as it was in the time of Nero in Rome. Once as I was nearly through the canvas a pair of strong hands caught me by the ankles, yanked me out and threw me for a fall, and a voice told me I could get going.

I walked around to the sideshow. There out front as a free show I saw the man with the elastic skin. He would pull it out from his face and neck and it would snap back into place. There I saw the tattooed man with fish, birds, brunette girls, ships, and many other shapes inked deep into his skin—and there too the Oriental Dancing Girl smiling to some giggling farmhands.

The spieler, a man with a thick upcurled mustache, turned to the crowd and let go in a smooth, loud voice: "La-deez and gen-tul-men, beneath yon canvas we have the curi-aw-si-ties and the monstraw-si-ties—the Wild Man of Borneo, the smallest dwarf ever seen of mankind and the tallest giant that ever came into existence, the most marvelous snake ever brought to your fair city, a man-eating python captured in the darkest jungles of Africa ever penetrated by man. And I would call your particular attention to Jo Jo, the dogfaced boy born forty miles from land and forty miles from sea. The price of admission, la-deez and gen-tul-men, is a dime, ten cents only, the tenth part of a dollar. Buy your tickets now before the big rush comes."

I had a dime and a nickel. With the dime, I bought a ticket. I went in and I saw the Wild Man of Borneo was a sad little shrimp and his whiskers messy. The Fat Woman, the Dwarf, the Giant seemed to me to be mistakes God had made, that God was absentminded when he shaped them. I hung around the midget and his wife, watched them sign their names to photographs they sold at ten cents—and they were so pleasant and witty that I saw I had guessed wrong about them and they were having more fun out of life than some of the men in the Q. shops.

I stood a long while watching the Giant and noticed he was quiet and satisfied about things. If a smarty asked, "How's the weather up there?" he might lift one eyebrow and let it pass, for he had heard it often enough. Nor did I feel sorry for the python. He may have been a man-eater but he was sleeping as if he had forgotten whoever it was he had swallowed and digested. After a third or fourth time around, the only one I felt sorry for was the Wild Man of Borneo. He could have been the only lonely creature among all the freaks. The Oriental Dancing Girl certainly was no freak, an average good-looking showgirl, somewhat dark of skin and probably a gypsy.

Later it came over me that at first sight of the

freaks I was sad because I was bashful. Except at home and among playmates, it didn't come easy for me to be looked at. I would pass people on the street and when they had gone by, I would wonder if they had turned their heads for another look at me. Walking down a church aisle between hundreds of people, I had a feeling of eyes on me. This was silly, but when you're bashful you have that feeling of eyes following you and boring through you. And there at the sideshow were these people, the freaks—and the business, the work, of each one of them was to be looked at. Every week, day by day, they sat or stood up to be looked at by thousands of people and they were paid to be looked at. If some one of them was more looked at than any others there was danger of jealousy on the part of those who didn't get looked at as much as they wished. Only the Wild Man of Borneo and the python seemed to be careless about whether anyone looked at them or not.

I walked out of the sideshow with my nickel still in my pocket. I passed the cane stand where a man held out rings and spoke like his tongue was oiled, "Only ten cents for a ring and the cane you ring is the cane you get." I stopped where a man was cheerfully calling with no letup, "Lem-o-nade, ice-cold lem-o-nade, a nice cool refreshing drink for a nickel, five cents, the twentieth part of a dollar." I passed by him to hear a laughing voice, "Here's where you get your hot roasted peanuts, those big double-jointed humpbacked peanuts, five a sack." I passed him by and still had my nickel.

Then I came to a man sitting on the ground, a deep-chested man with a face that had quiet on it and wouldn't bawl at you. I noticed he was barefoot. I looked up from his bare feet to see only stumps of arms at his shoulders. Between the first two toes of his right foot he held a card and lifted it toward me and said, "Take it and read it." I read in perfect handwriting, "I can write your name for you on a card for you to keep. The charge is only ten cents." I said, "I would if I had the ten cents. All I've got is a nickel." I took out the nickel and turned my pockets inside out and showed him that besides the nickel there was only a knife, a piece of string, and a buckeye. He took the nickel in his left foot. He put a pen between the first two toes of his right foot and on the card wrote "Charles A. Sandburg," lifted the foot up toward me, and I took the card. It was the prettiest my name had ever been written. His face didn't change. All the time it kept that quiet look that didn't strictly belong with a circus. I was near crying. I said some kind of thanks and picked up my feet and ran.

The Hangout

There was a row of buildings running west from
Chambers Street on the north side of Berrien. On
the corner stood the wooden grocery building of
"Swan H. Olson & Bro." Swan had a red chin beard,
always neatly trimmed, and waited on customers
quietly and politely. He had arrived from Sweden
in 1854, twenty years old, worked on Knox County

farms, enlisted in 1862, fought in the Atlanta campaign, marched with Sherman to the sea, across the Carolinas and on up to Washington for the Grand Review. Not until later years when I studied the marches and campaigns in which Swan Olson served did I come to a full respect for him. He was a foot soldier whose feet had taken him more than two thousand miles. He had been in wild and bloody battles, had waded creeks and rivers and marched in heavy rains day after day carrying rifle and blanket roll—but you couldn't tell it by seeing him measuring a quart of cranberries for Mrs. Nelson or hanging out a stockfish in front of the store on a winter morning to let the Swedes know their favorite holiday seafood had arrived.

His brother William, with the most elegantly spreading and curled red mustache in the Seventh Ward, was more of a talker than Swan. Both brothers hung their coats in the back of the store and put on black sleeves up to the elbows to keep their cuffs clean when they dipped into coffee sacks or dusty bins. Like all grocers, they fastened strong wire screens over the tops of apple baskets. At times one or two boys would watch inside the store and when the two brothers were busy with customers they would signal a boy outside who worked the wire screen loose and would run off with as many apples as his pockets and hat could hold.

I was six or seven when I learned a lesson about dealing at the Olson store. After Will Olson had wrapped what I was sent for, I handed him the book mother had given me and told him, "Put it on the book." He wrote in the book and handed it back to me. Then I asked how much would be a stick of licorice that caught my eye. "Five cents," said Will Olson and I said, "Put it on the book." Until then I had never bought anything for more than a penny. Now I had found a way to get something for nothing. I walked home hoping I would be sent often to the grocery with "the book." When I got home they saw my lips and chin black with licorice and asked about it. I said the grocery man gave me a big stick of licorice. "Did you pay him for it? Where did you get the money?" "I told him to put it on the book." It was then I heard the book was for the family, and not for me to be a mean little pig. My mother gave me a slap and told me, "Go and wash your dirty face," saying further that if it happened again I would get a licking I would remember.

On payday my father would take the book to the Olson store and they would figure up what he owed for the past month's groceries. After he paid they would give him a sack of candy for the children and a five-cent cigar for himself. He smoked an inch or two of the cigar each Sunday and it lasted till the next payday, when he got another cigar. The only smoking he ever did was these payday cigars. He couldn't waste them, so he smoked them.

There was an alley next to the Olsons' wooden building. Then came a one-story brick building where Franz Nelson ran a butcher shop. Here we would stop in and ask Franz when he was going to do some butchering. We liked to go with him to the slaughterhouse southeast of town and watch him knock a sledge into the head of a steer or stick a knife into the neck of a hog. At first we shivered at seeing the blood gushing from the slit in the hog's throat— then we got used to it. We helped at bringing water and carrying things to Franz and we watched him cutting steaks and chops on a tree-trunk chopping block. He gave us calf or beef liver to take home, and when a customer asked, "How about a piece of liver?" Franz would hand over liver without charge. He was freehanded with us boys when it came to baloney. We cut what we wanted and stood around eating it.

Next to the Franz Nelson butcher shop, in the same brick building, was our favorite hangout, the Julius Schulz cigar shop. In the front room were a wide aisle and two glass showcases filled with Schulz-

made cigars and a line of pipes and smoking to-
baccos. Mr. Schulz we didn't see often; he was out
drumming up trade. He was medium-sized, wore a
heavy brown mustache and matching it a brown suit
and a brown derby, a gold watch chain on his brown
vest. He would come into the store, look over his
account books, fill a valise with samples, and go
away without a look at us kids whether there were
two, five, or six of us hanging around. We all liked
Mr. Schulz. He didn't know our names nor bother
to speak to us, but summer or winter he let us hang
around and use his place for a kind of clubroom.

The back room was the main hangout. There sat
"Nig" Bohnenberger, whose folks spoke German but
he hadn't learned it. "They got to calling me Nig
because I'm dark-complected," he said. He had a
hawk nose, a pale face, a thin body, and a mind
that was always thinking things over. He read the
papers and while he rolled cigars and licked the
wrappers he told us what was wrong with the country
and the town. He often ended what he said with,
"Of that I can tell you I'm pos-i-tive." He liked to
be positive and we liked him being pos-i-tive. We
saw him in coughing spells and slowly fade away
from consumption. One boy came from Nig's funeral
saying, "He looked so natural in the coffin I couldn't
keep from crying."

To the cigar shop came the boys in the between-times of work and play. In warmer weather on nights and Sundays when the cigar store was closed, we met on the sidewalk in front and sang. There was tall, skinny, bony John Hultgren, a Swede boy who worked in the Boyer broom factory, and chubby, cheek-puffed, bright-eyed John Kerrigan, an Irish lad learning the plumber's trade under his father—both of them tenors. There was Willis ("Bohunk") Calkins and myself who were fair at baritone and bass. This quartet could give "In the Evening by the Moonlight," "Swanee River," "Carry Me Back to Old Virginia," "I Found a Horseshoe"—and we said we were good and when Al Field's Minstrels came to town they ought to hear us. Bohunk a couple of nights brought his banjo.

One morning about nine I drifted into the Schulz store to find excitement. In the night someone had broken open a back window and taken what money there was, maybe eight or ten dollars. Heavy rain had been falling all night. The thief, it was said, probably counted on few people being on the street and they would be hurrying through the rain, not stopping to look in on the store. We had been reading Old Cap Collier and Nick Carter and we tried sleuthing for clues. We hoped to find something the thief had dropped, but he hadn't dropped anything.

There was mud on the floor from his shoes when he stepped in from the window and then less and less mud on a line toward the money drawer—but not a clue!

Soon came a short man with quiet eyes and a fine black mustache. He wore a blue suit, with a star on his coat. We knew him but had never seen him working on a case. He was Marshal Hinman, chief of police, and he had with him one of his best uniformed policemen. We watched them work and we saw that inside the store they didn't find any more clues than we did. Then they stepped out the back door and went to work on what we had missed. There in the black mud were shoe tracks. Marshal Hinman studied the shoe tracks. His face was sober and earnest as he looked down into the mud. I was thinking, "Now I'm watching a real man hunter at work."

The marshal called for some cardboard and was handed an empty shoe box. He took the top of the box, pulled a knife from his pocket, and laying the shoe-box top over a shoe track in the mud he cut the cardboard to the shape of the thief's shoe sole. Then we saw him crouching again over another shoe track. He was slow and patient, I noticed, like all good sleuths and man hunters. His knife cut the shoe-box bottom to the shape of another shoe track in the mud. It came to me like a flash what he was doing. The first cardboard he cut was the left shoe and the second one was the right shoe of the thief. After this was over he studied the tracks some more and went inside the store again. Unless his keen eyes had caught some clue he wasn't telling us about, we could see that all he had to work on was to find some man whose shoes were the same left and right sizes as his cardboard cuttings. I reasoned to myself that it wouldn't do for him to stop a thousand people on Main Street and try his cardboard cuttings on their shoe bottoms. There would be maybe fifty or a hundred men wearing exactly that size shoe and since it had been a rainy night, they would know where they had been out of the rain and every one would prove an alibi.

We hoped Marshal Hinman would catch the thief. We saw him leave after saying, "We haven't got much to work on but we'll do the best we can." Then time went by and the years passed and the case was never solved.

From the Schulz store we went sometimes next door west into a cubbyhole of a house—one room maybe twelve feet by twelve. Here sat a man with a leather apron and a line of tools and leather in easy reach. We watched him cut leather for the half-sole of a shoe or boot, then fill his mouth with wooden pegs and, taking one peg at a time from his mouth, fit and hammer them into holes he made with an awl. Or if the customer wanted the half-sole stitched in, John Swedenborg could do it, carefully waxing the heavy threads before he stitched. He could glue a patch on or sew it, depending on what he thought was needed. He liked his work and was steady at it from eight in the morning till six in the evening. We looked in on him more often in the winter when his little place with its coal stove was cozy.

He was a long man with stooped shoulders, with a good face when quiet, and burning eyes and trembling lips when he spoke. Always John spoke to us the same lesson, keeping silence only when his mouth was filled with wooden pegs. I learned later the word for John. He was a Zealot. His zeal ran in every drop of his blood. So many times we heard him say: "I have Yesus in my heart. Yesus is with me all the time. I pray to my Yesus in the daytime and in the nighttime. You boys will never go wrong if you can get Yesus in your heart. He is my Saviour and He can be your Saviour. He is the Light of the World. When I have Him I am not afraid. I cannot be afraid, for He has told me to lean on Him when it is dark and things go wrong. You should learn to pray to Him, boys. You should learn to kneel at His blessèd feet and ask forgiveness and ask Him to take you in His arms." He had his own style of speaking straight from the heart.

The words would come from John Swedenborg with his eyes having a fire in them and his lips shaking as he shaped the words: "We are not long for this world. My Yesus is waiting for me in the next world and it will be blessèd to see Him." He lived sober, went to Wednesday evening prayer meetings and special services, and took his family to church Sunday morning and night. We saw him several times in coughing spells. There were days his shop was closed. His end, like Nig Bohnenberger's next door, came from consumption. Neither of them was afraid to go but John was more sure than Nig that he was going where he would have more shining happiness than he ever had on earth.

8

The Dirty Dozen

One Sunday afternoon a bunch of us came together in front of the Olson store, most of us about sixteen or seventeen. We were going to have a photograph made. We counted and there were twelve of us. Someone said, "Then we can show people what the Dirty Dozen looks like." And the name Dirty Dozen stuck. It sounded like we were a gang and went in for gang fights. But the Dirty Dozen never fought

another gang nor did we have any fights among ourselves. Seven of the twelve were sons of Americans
from Sweden. Four were "native American." One
was the son of a Frenchman.

Ed Rosenberg should have been counted with
the Dirty Dozen. It was they who worked out his
nickname. He was pale and slim, a little undersized,
always cheery and with his own sense of humor. He
muffed an easy fly once and from then on we called
him "Muff," or more often "Muffa." When running
a race on a cinder path one day he stumbled and
fell and got up saying, "I hit de grit." From then
on it was "Muffa de Grit." He knocked in a winning
run in a ball game and strutted around with his head
high crying, "Who won the game? Eddie Ampa!
Eddie Ampa!" Where he picked up the "Ampa" we
didn't know but it sounded right, and now his name
was "Muffa de Grit Eddie Ampa." Out of some sidewalk scuffling with a bigger fellow Eddie came saying, "He gave me de grunt." So for a long while
whenever Ed Rosenberg was seen coming to join
the bunch he heard them calling all together, "Here
comes Muffa de Grit Eddie Ampa de Grunt." We
missed him when he went over to Moline to work
in the Deere plow factory, where they called him
by his right name.

Charles ("Frenchy") Juneau was one of the best

chums I had. His father was a short, sturdy man with a head and beard like you see in portraits of Victor Hugo. And Frenchy himself had something of the Napoleon face and head. He could pull a lock of black hair down his forehead, stick his right hand into his coat below the lapels, and ask, "If I'm not Napoleon, who am I?" He had worked as a metal polisher in a stove factory in Aurora and when the works shut down he came to his father's home in Galesburg, held down several jobs he didn't like, and after a time went back to Aurora as a metal polisher when the stove factory opened again. He didn't care for books nor singing as I did but he had brightness and drollery and when we had nothing to talk about it was good just being together. We would go downtown, walk Main Street, buy a half-dozen cream puffs for a dime, walk Main Street eating our cream puffs, walk around the Public Square, and back to Berrien Street calling it a merry evening.

We went together to see William Jennings Bryan get off a train and get on a platform on Mulberry Street next to the Q. tracks and make a speech. Later when Bryan was speaking in Monmouth, sixteen miles from Galesburg on the Q., we rode the cowcatcher of an engine on a cold October night. We were chilled through and Frenchy bought a pint of blackberry brandy which warmed us. This was the only time we went in for booze. After we heard Bryan speak, we rode an engine cowcatcher back to Galesburg, and we went back to our old ways of walking Main Street eating cream puffs.

We went that fall to a big tent on the Knox campus and heard Bob Ingersoll give a speech lambasting the Democrats and Free Silver. But first Frenchy and I went for a sack of cream puffs, and standing on the edge of the crowd we listened to the famous Republican orator from Peoria and munched our cream puffs. One night when the bakery was out of cream puffs we tried chocolate éclairs and decided, "Never again if we can get cream puffs."

There was a summer Sunday afternoon that eight of the Dirty Dozen could never forget. We had met in front of Schulz's, the sun pouring down hot and sweltering. Someone said, "Let's go out to that pond on the Booth farm and have a swim." On the way, just inside the city limits, we came to the "Old Brick," as we called it, a pond about thirty yards long by twenty yards wide. Once a small brickyard had been there and it was all gone except the pond and a big wheel we used to dive from. The water at its deepest was up to our shoulders, and the bottom was slushy mud with broken bricks and pieces of tile and glass. We had grown tired of it and we had heard that the people in the new homes built near-by didn't like to have the boys swimming so close. But it was nearly three miles to the Booth farm pond and we decided on this hot day we would have our swim in the Old Brick. We peeled off our clothes. All of us had stepped into the water except slow Ed Rosenberg. Then came the surprise. "Look!" yelled one of the boys, "there's Wiley!"

On Day Street we saw the patrol wagon and coming toward us big Policeman Frank Peterson and big Chief Wiley. The chief had his right hand raised and he was hollering, "Stay where you are, you're under arrest!" As he came closer we heard, "You boys ought to know you're not allowed to swim here. It's against the law and every one of you will get into the wagon and come along with me." We got into part of our clothes and finished dressing in the patrol wagon—all of us except Ed Rosenberg. He had grabbed his pants and shirt and the last seen of him he was nearly out of sight hot-footing it along the Narrow Gauge Railroad.

The patrol wagon had no top, and the seats ran lengthwise. Four of us sat on one side, three on the other, looking at each other and wondering, taking side glances at Wiley and Peterson at the wagon end. We were going to be hauled along streets where people knew us—arrested and on the way to the calaboose! And after a night in the calaboose we would be taken to court and there would be a trial and we wondered what would be the worst they could do to us—how did we know? The law is the law and anything can happen in the law. There was my nice brother Mart opposite me—the first time any Sandburg in Galesburg had been arrested! There were Bohunk Calkins and "Jiddy" Ericson and Charlie Bloomgreen from their nice homes and decent people on Berrien Street, now in a wagon watched by two policemen, being hauled in broad daylight to the Cherry Street calaboose.

Along Main Street we didn't see anybody we knew who knew us. At the calaboose we were locked up, three of us in one cell where four drunks were sobering up and the other four in a cell where three drunks were sobering up. There were no chairs, no cots; you sat on the stone floor or kept standing. It was about three o'clock when they locked us up. It was seven, when they were getting ready to feed the drunks, that they unlocked our cells and said we could go home. And they said more, "You're under orders to appear in court tomorrow morning before Justice of the Peace Holcomb at ten o'clock."

We walked to our Berrien Street homes, talking all the way about what Justice Holcomb would hand us in the morning. Most of us believed the justice wouldn't give us jail sentences but maybe he would give us light fines, "two dollars and costs." When Tom Beckum or Peg Hoey got their names in the papers for being drunk and disorderly Justice Holcomb fined them "two dollars and costs." The costs were five dollars and some of us wondered where we would dig up such money. I could pay the fine but not the costs. And I couldn't tell beforehand what my father would say if Mart or I told him, "You've got to let me have five dollars for costs or a son of August Sandburg goes to jail."

We stood before Justice Holcomb the next morning. We pleaded guilty to the charge that we had stripped naked and gone swimming in an old brickyard pond inside the city limits on yesterday's Sunday afternoon. Justice Holcomb gave us a talk like he was a good uncle of ours; we should understand it was against the law to do what we did. And he had us each promise we would never again go swimming in that pond.

We walked away, glad to be free and footloose again. What we agreed on was, "They didn't have to arrest us and throw us in that wagon and take us to the lockup. Not one of us had heard there was any law about not swimming in that pond. Why didn't they put up a sign 'Against the law to swim here'? We have been swimming in that pond for years. If they had just got out of their wagon and told us we were breaking the law every one of us would have promised never to swim there again. What's the matter with the police?"

At home father and mother were quiet and decent about the whole affair. They didn't say so but they seemed to agree with us that the law and the police had been somewhat silly. Policeman Frank Peterson, who was with Chief Wiley, was then renting the second-story rooms of our house. I think Peterson, if he had been acting on his own, would have talked to us and given us warnings instead of hollering like Wiley, "Stay where you are, you're under arrest!" If you're a grown man and you hear a police chief say, "You're under arrest," it gives you at least a little shiver. And if you're sixteen there is something terrorizing about it—unless you're what they call an Old Offender who has been to reform schools.

I still refuse to feel the slightest guilt, and I am sure Muffa de Grit would agree with me. He ran out the Narrow Gauge Railroad till the police wagon was out of sight, put on his pants and shirt, sneaked back to the Old Brick, picked up his stockings, shoes and hat, and went home. He half expected the police would come for him but they didn't. The case wasn't that important. We all handed it to Muffa de Grit. He had quick wits and was fast on his feet.

Fellows two to four years older were putting on a dance once a month, renting a hall and hiring two fiddlers, and they picked for themselves the name of the Golden Rod Club. Husky Larson, Jiddy Ericson, and others of the Dirty Dozen said we could match the Golden Rod outfit, and we rented a hall and paid a couple of fiddlers. It came to twenty-five cents apiece each night we danced. We decided to call ourselves the Monarch Club. A fiddler called the quadrilles, and between we danced the waltz, two-step, polka, and schottische with the Hanson sisters, Allie Harshbarger, Gertie Gent, and other lovely girls. The fiddlers played the sad "Home Sweet Home" at eleven o'clock.

Fatty Beckman, Skinny Seeley, and I were the craziest at baseball. We began playing earlier in the spring and kept on later in the fall than the other boys—till the first frosts came and the last russet apple had fallen from the tree at the back fence of the pasture. We began playing earlier in the morning and played later in the evening than the others. Fatty wasn't fat; his cheeks puffed out a little. And Skinny wasn't skinny; he was merely lean and hard. I was

"Cully," I suppose because it was considered an improvement on "Charlie." Fatty Beckman was the son of a widow and in September took days off from ballplaying to haul a wagon from house to house selling cabbages at five cents a head, earning fifty to sixty cents a day and jingling a pocket full of nickels when he came to the pasture for a last hour before supper. Skinny began hanging around the Auditorium, the new theater, helping the stage carpenter "Husky" Johnson, and the property man "Cully" Rose. They trained him so when he went to Chicago he caught on as a stagehand.

The time came when I found other chums with different interests. There was Willis Calkins, a half-block away at Pearl and Berrien, his father a trolley-car motorman, clean and kindly, with a laughter for all weathers, his mother a beautiful woman whom we saw in one short year fade away from consumption. Willis was their only child. They were a singing family with Kentucky ancestors. Willis played the banjo, showed me the chords and how to accompany songs.

My first musical instrument had been a willow whistle I cut for myself. The pencil between the teeth and the tune rapped out by the right thumb followed. Then came the comb with paper over it and the mouth vocalizing—not so good. The ten-cent kazoo was better; you could imitate, in crude fashion, either a brass band or a rooster. A tin fife, a wooden flageolet, were interesting, and the ocarina surpassed all the wind instruments I fooled with. My first string instrument was a cigar box banjo for which I cut and turned pegs and strung the wires myself; neither tunes nor chords could be coaxed from it. A slightly disabled concertina, at fifty cents from Mr. Gumbiner's New York Pawn Shop on Main Street, came next, developed wheezes, and was discarded. I tried the Old Man's accordion and it wheezed too often. Then came a two-dollar banjo from Mr. Gumbiner. This was a honey and from Willis I learned the chords. From the gracious Mrs. Schwartz on Ferris Street I had three banjo lessons at twenty-five cents a lesson. I should have gone on but it was Hard Times.

Willis could give the national popular songs, minstrel ditties, old ballads. He had a smooth baritone voice and put an easy charm into his singing. He had a long nose on a horse face, his good humor was irresistible, and he was welcome at all parties. He had a lumbering torso and a rolling gait. Someone nicknamed him "Bohunk" and it stuck.

One summer Bohunk and I walked a dozen times the three miles south and east to the pond on the Booth farm for the swimming there, "water up to your chin." It was in these fields out near town that we saw timothy hay growing, and oats and wheat. It was Indian corn, though, that hit me deepest. There was sweet corn for corn on the cob at the dinner table and there were acres of broomcorn and sorghum. But the Indian corn stood tallest and ran for miles on miles, food for men and horses, and there was a wonder about the little, white, soft ears of June becoming the tough, yellow, hard, and husky ears of late September that could lie on the frozen ground and wait to be used. We saw old zigzag rail fences go down and the Osage-orange hedge take its place. I picked hedge branches with the right crook to them and cut with a jackknife the club I wanted for playing shinny.

Walking back from the Booth farm pond Bohunk and I would make a decision where Farnham Street crossed the Peoria tracks. We could bear to the left, make a short cut across the Lombard campus, and on a hot day take a big cool drink of water from a cast-iron dipper chained to the Lombard pump. Or we could take a long walk on Farnham to Brooks Street and steal some luscious eating apples from Jon W. Grubb's orchard, tucking our pockets full and circling our shirts over the waistband of the pants with a line of apples. The question we discussed at Farnham and the Peoria tracks was simple:

"What'll it be? A shortcut and a drink or a long walk and apples?"

When the Calkins family moved out the Sjodins moved in—Swedes who had lived in Chicago fifteen years and lost their Swedish accent. Mr. Sjodin was a journeyman tailor, could measure, cut, and sew a suit of clothes. He walked with his head high and his shoulders erect and thrown back as if to say, "I am a free man and I bow to no masters or overlords. I cringe before no man." He was the first real radical I knew. He wanted a new society, a new world where no man had to cringe before another. He was an anarchist, a Populist, and a Socialist, at home with anyone who was against the government and the plutocrats who rob the poor. He was a skilled tailor who took good care of his wife, one daughter, and two sons and liked nothing better than a few glasses of beer with plenty of talk about politics and the coming revolution.

John Sjodin was two or three years older than I and had worked two years in a Milwaukee Avenue department store in Chicago. He had taken three lessons in clog dancing and from him I learned three steps to clog and never forgot them. He had absorbed much of Chicago's vivid and reckless flair and could give the feel of it in his talk. He had read widely.

We lay on the grass next to the ditch in front of his home on summer nights. He could talk on and on about the exploits of a detective named Macon Moore. We both rated Macon Moore higher than Old Cap Collier and Nick Carter.

With John Sjodin and his brother Albert, another boy, and Mart, I chipped in and we bought one bonerack horse for two dollars and another for three dollars. We hitched them to light wagons we borrowed, drove some fifty miles to the Illinois River between Peoria and Chillicothe opposite Spring Green, where we camped, fished, and went swimming. The three-dollar horse died on us and we buried him with respect and many jokes. We scraped our pockets and raised five dollars that bought us another horse for the trip home to Galesburg, where we sold it for three dollars to the man who had sold us the three-dollar horse that died. The man who sold us the two-dollar horse wouldn't let us sell it back to him and I forget what we did with it, though we spoke highly of it as a willing horse that had staying power.

John at that time could be jolly, liked jokes and funny stories and had plenty of them. He was, like his father, a hard-and-fast political-action radical. "The big corporations" were running the country, as John saw it, and the time would come when the working people, farmers and laborers, would organize and get political power and take over the big corporations, beginning with the government ownership of railroads. Always John was sensitive about the extremes of the rich and the poor, the poor never knowing what tomorrow would bring and the rich having more than they knew what to do with.

I never saw John in a fight and I know he wouldn't have made any kind of a leader of a mob or riot. He would argue his points with anybody but he wouldn't let an argument or a debate run into a quarrel. He had his own reverence for life and said many a time that he couldn't hate a millionaire and most of the rich were sorry fools who didn't know what to do with their money except to put it to work making more money.

I asked John many questions and he nearly always had answers. I didn't argue with him. He believed deeply in a tide of feeling among the masses of the people. This tide would grow and become stronger and in generations to come the American people would challenge and break the power of the corporations, the interests of special privilege. John was not yet a voter but he favored the People's Party, the Populists. His main influence on me was to start me thinking. He made me know I ought to know more about what was going on in politics, industry, business, and crime over the widespread American scene.

9

First Paydays

I was eleven when I had the first regular job that
paid me cash. There had been odd jobs for earning
money and Saturdays and after school hours we took
gunny sacks and went around streets, alleys, barns,
and houses hunting in ditches and rubbish piles for
rags, bones, scrap iron, and bottles, for which cash
was paid us, my gunny sack one week bringing me
eighteen cents. Now I was wearing long pants and
every Friday was payday.

My employer was the real estate firm of Callender & Rodine on the second floor of a building on Main midway between Kellogg and Prairie. Mr. Callender was a heavy man with a large blond mustache. His head was wide between the ears and he had a smooth, round "bay window." Mr. Rodine was lean and had a pink face with blue eyes.

Their office was large and I would guess it was ten paces from the west wall where Mr. Callender had his desk to the east wall where Mr. Rodine also had a big rolltop desk with pigeonholes to stick papers in. It was Mr. Callender who told me about pigeonholes and what they are for. It came into my head, but I didn't mention it to Mr. Callender, that some of the pigeonholes were so thin you couldn't find a pigeon that could fly into one. Nor did I mention to him that it would be fun to bring in five or six pigeons and put them in the pigeonholes so that when Mr. Callender and Mr. Rodine rolled back the tops of their desks first thing in the morning, the office would be full of pigeons flapping and fluttering. This idea I liked to roll around in my head and I told other boys about it. One boy said, "If you did that, they would prosecute you." We made him tell us what it is to be prosecuted and for several weeks we saluted him, "Hello, Prosecutor" or "Here's Little Prosecutor again."

Mr. Callender and Mr. Rodine treated me fair. The longest talk I had with either of them was when Mr. Callender told me what my work was to be. After that, for month after month, about the only talk between us was on Friday morning when Mr. Callender handed me my pay, saying, "Here you are," and I said, "Thanks," and skipped.

They gave me a key to the office and I unlocked the door about a quarter to eight each morning, Monday through Friday. I swept the office, digging in for the dust in the corners and every crack in the floorboards, then sweeping the dust out into the hall and along the hall six or eight feet to the top of the wide stairway leading to the street. Reaching the bottom of the stairs I swept the accumulations of my earnest and busy broom onto the sidewalk of Main Street and across the sidewalk. With two or three grand final strokes I swept a half bushel of dust and paper and string and cigar butts out on the cobblestones to join other sweepings and layers of horse droppings. If a strong east wind was blowing, it would be no time until my sweepings were scattered all along Main Street.

Back upstairs, I carried the brass spittoon that stood at Mr. Callender's desk out in the hall to a cubbyhole with a faucet and running cold water. I dumped, washed, rinsed, and rinsed again and took the honorable and serviceable spittoon back to its place at Mr. Callender's desk. Then I did the same cleaning of Mr. Rodine's spittoon. About once in six or eight weeks I polished the spittoons till they were bright and shining.

This morning service of mine for Callender & Rodine took less than a half hour. I was pleased and thankful when on Friday morning Mr. Callender would bring his right hand out of a pocket and, with a look on his face as though he had almost forgotten it, hand me a coin with "Here you are." And I would take the coin, say "Thanks," skip down the stairway, and on the sidewalk open my hand to look at what it held. There it was, twenty-five cents, a silver quarter of a dollar.

On the second floor a few doors west of the Callender & Rodine office was the printing press and office of the *Galesburg Republican-Register*, to which we carrier boys went as soon as school let out at half-past three. As the papers came off the flatbed press, we took them to a table and folded them. When I had folded the fifty or sixty papers for my route, I took them to a man who counted them again to make sure my count was correct, with one "extra" for myself. If a single paper seemed a little thick, the man would look to see whether one paper had been stuck inside of another, a trick some boys worked too often. Then with a bundle of papers under my arm, I went down the stairs to Main Street, turned north at the next corner, and went up Prairie Street. I learned how to cross-fold a paper so it could be thrown spang against a front door. If a house was near enough, I didn't have to leave the sidewalk to make my throw. On Prairie Street, however, the rich and the well-to-do lived, most of their houses set back so far from the sidewalk that I had to walk in halfway or more before making my throw.

At one house set well back a man would often be at home and expecting me—more yet, expecting the latest telegraphed news over America and the wide world. He would step out of the door to take the paper from my hand, the most roly-poly fat man in town. He was round everywhere you looked at him—a waddly barrel of a man, with a double chin, a round face, a gray mustache and goatee. This was the Honorable Clark E. Carr, mentioned often as the Republican Party boss of Knox County and having a hand in national politics. He had been appointed postmaster by Republican Presidents. He was to serve as United States Minister to Denmark.

Having left Mr. Carr with the latest news about how President Cleveland and the Democrats were ruining the country, I went along Prairie Street and threw a paper on the front porch of the biggest house in town. People said, "It cost more than any house ever put up in Galesburg, eighty thousand dollars." It was gray stone, three stories, with towers and fancy curves. Here lived the Honorable George A. Lawrence. He married a good woman who had a big fortune. He was a lawyer with brown sideburns that stood out and waved and shook in a strong wind.

I went on with my papers to the end of Prairie Street, went a block west to Cherry, turned south to Main, and had one copy of the *Republican-Register* left to take home. I had walked about two miles. When there was mud or snow or stormy weather it took about an hour and a half to carry my route and in good weather about an hour and a quarter. The *Republican-Register* paid me one dollar a week. I was more than satisfied with that weekly silver dollar.

Walking between rows of houses, many of them set widely apart—wider lots than at a later time—I came to know yards and trees—trees that I had seen in sun and rain in summer, and cloud and snow in winter, branches bending down with ice on them. Here and there in a backyard would be a tomato patch and carrots asking to be pulled out of the ground. Some yards had apple trees, and I helped myself to the windfalls.

For the little building in every backyard some said "backhouse," some said "privy." Carrying newspapers and later slinging milk I saw all the different styles of backhouses—the clean, roomy, elegant ones with latticework in front, those with leaky roofs and loose boards where the cold rain and wind came through, a few with soft paper that had no printing, but mostly it was newspapers neatly cut, or catalogues. When you had to go to the backhouse you stepped out into the weather—in rain or sleet. If the thermometer said zero you left your warm spot near the stove and the minute you were out the back door the cold put a crimp and a shiver in you.

About once a year a Negro we called Mister Elsey would come in the night with his wagon and clean the vault of our privy. He lived on Pine Street in a house he owned. We had respect for him and called him Mister. His work was always done at night. He came and went like a shadow in the moon.

I came to know the houses and yards of Prominent People. Their names were often in the paper. When they left for Kewanee, Peoria, or Chicago, I would read a "personal" about it in the paper. And

I would notice the green blinds pulled over the front windows and three or four days of my papers waiting for them on the front porch when they came back from Kewanee, Peoria, or Chicago. If snow or rain was blowing in on the porch floor I would pull the doormat over the papers and have a feeling that I was not completely useless.

I had seen at his work one morning the man who went up and down Main Street and got the "personals," a short man with sandy hair, thin sandy sideburns, and a freckled face. He was writing in a notebook. I went closer and heard him asking a man how names were spelled. He thanked the man, put the book in his pocket, and went into Kellogg & Drake's drygoods store. There I saw him speaking to Ed Drake, with the notebook again in his left hand as he wrote. Mr. Callender happening along, I asked him who was the man writing names in a book. "That's Fred Jeliff, reporter for the *Republican-Register*," said Mr. Callender.

I was fascinated. I could see Fred Jeliff walking back to the *Republican-Register* office and sitting at a table to write with a lead pencil on the same kind of paper the *Republican-Register* was printed on. Then he would carry the sheets to the man they called a "typesetter," and when the *Republican-Register* for that day was printed the names would be spelled like Fred Jeliff wrote them in his note-book up and down Main Street. I believed you could be a newspaper reporter if you could spell names and write them with a pencil on paper.

A year came when I was deep in the newspaper business. In addition to the afternoon route of the *Republican-Register* at a dollar a week, I carried a morning route of Chicago papers at seventy-five cents a week. Every morning, weekday and Sunday, I was on a Q. depot platform when the Fast Mail train from Chicago came in at seven-ten. Out of a mail car as the train slowed to a stop rolled the bundles we picked up and carried across Seminary Street to the front of the Crocker & Robbins grocery where a covered platform kept rain or snow off us.

We were working for Mr. Edwards, who had a store on Main Street where he sold books and sta-tionery and kept a newsstand. He had long red whis-kers and a Santa Claus look if he wasn't excited. When he told us what to do he wasn't bossy or fussed up. When two or three boys started scuffing he would step in like a mother hen who was going to have peace and no blood spilled.

We cut the ropes from the bundles, and there fresh as summer-morning dew or winter-daybreak frost were the *Chicago Tribune, Chicago Record,*

Chicago Inter-Ocean, Chicago Times, Chicago Herald, and *Chicago Chronicle.* Each boy got his papers and started on his route, knowing well what he would catch if he threw a Democratic *Chicago Times* on the porch of a house where they were paying for the Republican *Chicago Tribune.* Where the other papers were two cents a copy, the *Chicago Record,* started by Victor Lawson, was one cent. You couldn't tell whether a man was taking the *Record* because it was cheapest or because it was the only Chicago paper independent in politics and giving what both sides had to say. When a house was taking two papers, one of them was the *Record.*

On the morning route I covered South and Mulberry streets and ended on Main. On Sunday mornings from seven-thirty till around noon, I pulled a little wagon of the Chicago papers, selling them at five cents a copy and getting one cent for myself out of each copy sold. I had about fifty regular customers and when there was extra-special big news, such as the assassination of Mayor Carter Harrison in Chicago, I sold ten or twenty more papers.

Along with the other boys I would end up about one o'clock at Mr. Edwards' store. After we turned in our money to Mr. Edwards, five or six of us would cross the street to a lunch counter. Always what we did was the same as the Sunday before. We climbed up on stools and each of us said with a grin, "One and a bun," meaning one fried egg laid between a split bun. We were hungry and we smacked and talked between bites of our five-cent snack. Each of us paid his nickel and felt chesty about it. It was like we were grown men and we had money we'd earned and could eat away from home. Some of us had pants that needed patching but we were little independent merchants spending a nickel of our profits.

What with spading two or three gardens, picking a pail or two of potato bugs, selling Pennsylvania Grit along Main Street, and other odd jobs, I made about twelve dollars a month. One odd job was "cleaning brick." A brick house or store torn down, we took trowels, knocked off the dried mortar and tried to make an old brick look new. Our pay ran so much a hundred of brick cleaned. I worked at it between my paper routes and averaged about fifteen cents an hour.

But it was more sport than work when we answered the cry, "The English sparrow must go!" The state was paying one cent for each dead English sparrow and I brought down more than thirty. I tried killing them with a "rubber gun" of my own make, a crotched stick with rubber bands holding a leather sling you put your stone in; then you pulled back the rubber, aimed at the sparrow, and let 'er go. Out of hundreds of rubber-gun shots I brought down one sparrow. Then I got an air rifle. I half believed a Swedish neighbor boy Axel Johnson when he said that an air rifle or a rubber gun was better for killing birds than a shotgun or a rifle using powder. "The birds can smell powder a mile off," said Axel, and he had me thinking hard about the smelling power of birds.

10

Milk Wagon Days

I was fourteen, near fifteen, in October of 1892. My mother would wake me at half-past five in the morning. She had ready for me when I came down from the garret a breakfast of buckwheat cakes, fried side pork, maybe applesauce or prunes, and coffee. I walked about two miles to the house and barn of George Burton, who had two milk wagons. I could have saved myself half the walk by taking a trolley but I saved instead the nickel carfare.

In this October were days I had a sore throat. I went to bed two days and sent word to Mr. Burton that I wasn't able to work. On reporting for work, I explained to him and he looked at me with suspicion and said not a word. I still had throat pains and was weak, but I didn't explain this to Mr. Burton; he looked suspicious enough.

That same week Mart went down with a sore throat and it was four days before he was up and around. Then the two youngest boys stayed in bed with throats so sore they couldn't eat. Freddie was two years old and Emil was seven. Emil had a broad freckled face, blue eyes, a quick beaming smile from a large mouth. He was strong for his age. He and I wrestled, scuffled, knocked off hats, and played tricks on each other. We liked the same stories and I read to him my favorites from the Grimm stories. He called often for "The Knapsack, the Hat, and the Horn."

We moved a narrow bed down to the kitchen, the one room that had a stove. Next to the west window, with afternoon sun pouring in, we put Emil and Freddie side by side in the bed, each with a throat looking queer. They seemed to be getting weaker, and though we knew it would be a dollar and a half for a call from Doctor Wilson, I walked to his Main Street office and told him to come as soon as he could.

Doctor Wilson came in about an hour, stepping into our kitchen in his elegant long black coat, white shirt and collar, and silk necktie. He had a good name as a doctor. He took a flat steel instrument from his case, put it on Emil's tongue and pressed down and looked keen and long at Emil's throat. He did the same for Freddie. Then Doctor Wilson stood up, turned to my father and mother and his face was sober and sorry as he said, "It is diphtheria."

Late that afternoon the city health commissioner nailed a big red card on our front door: DIPHTHERIA, warning people not to come to our house because it had a catching disease. I went to work next morning with a feeling that Mr. Burton wouldn't like it if I stayed home, that he would be suspicious like he was when I came back after two days off. I told him we had diphtheria at our house with a red card on the front door. He didn't say anything. So I went with my milk cans from one house to another across the town from seven in the morning till about one in the afternoon. The next two mornings again I peddled milk for Mr. Burton and there were houses where women were anxious, saying, "Do you think it right you should be handling our milk if you have diphtheria at your house?" I said I had told Mr. Burton about it, but he didn't say anything and I thought he wouldn't like it if I stayed home. And the women had worried faces and said, "It doesn't look right."

On the third day when Doctor Wilson made his third call, he said the boys were not making any improvement. He shook his head and said, "All we can do now is to hope. They might get better. They might get worse. I can't tell." Late that afternoon we were all there, with a west sun shining in on Emil and Freddie where they lay with their eyes closed. It was Freddie who first stopped breathing. Mother, touching his forehead and hands, her voice shaking and tears coming down her face, said, "He is cold. Our Freddie is gone." We watched Emil. He had had a rugged body and we hoped he might pull through. But his breathing came slower and in less than a half hour he seemed to have stopped breathing. Mother put her hands on him and said with her body shaking, "Oh God, Emil is gone too."

The grief hit us all hard. In the Front Room the marble-topped center table with the big Family Bible was moved to a corner. In its place were two small white caskets. Neighbors and friends came, some with flowers. The Kranses and the Holmeses came to look at the faces of their two little relations. The Reverend Carl A. Nyblad spoke the Swedish Lutheran service. A quartet sang "Jesus, Lover of My Soul." The undertaker moved here and there as though it was what he did every day. Mother cried, but it was a quiet crying and she didn't shake her shoulders like when she said, "Oh God, Emil is gone too." Mart and I didn't cry. We kept our eyes dry and our faces hard. For two nights we had cried before going to sleep and waking in the night we had cried more, and it was our secret why we weren't crying at a public funeral.

We saw the two little white caskets carried out the front door and put in the black hearse with glass windows at the sides and end, four black tassels on the top corners.

We followed in a closed carriage. At the grave we heard the words, "Ashes to ashes, dust to dust," saw the two little coffins lowered and a handful of earth dropped on them, the sober faces of the Kranses and the Holmeses having grains of comfort for us.

We were driven home in the closed carriage, father and mother, sisters Mary and Esther, Mart and I. We went into the house. It was all over. The clock had struck for two lives and would never strike again for them. Freddie hadn't lived long enough to get any tangles in my heart. But Emil I missed; for years I missed him and had my wonderings about what a chum he would have made.

There were two days I didn't report to George Burton for work in that diphtheria and burial week. When I did report to him he was like before, not a word, not even "Hard luck," or "Too bad." Mr. Burton had a lean face with a brown mustache he liked to twirl in his fingers—and a "retreating" chin. He had a beautiful wife and his face lighted up at the sight of her. He had two or three fast horses he liked to drive with a sulky. One was a yearling bred from a glossy black mare he owned. The mare had a small head and her thin scrawny neck didn't match her heavy body. Mr. Burton said she was pedigreed and had class yet about half the time he had her hitched to his milk wagon. He enjoyed clucking at her to get a burst of speed and then pulling her in.

After Emil and Freddie died, doctor and undertaker bills, the cemetery lot, took regular cuts out of the month's wages of my father. We were now a family of seven, and besides money for food, clothes, coal, schoolbooks, Papa had to make his payments or lose the house. And Mary in her third and last year of high school had to have better clothes than in the grade schools. The twelve dollars a month George Burton paid me came in handy for the family.

It was a hard winter and somehow I couldn't see my way to take out of my pay two dollars for a pair of felt boots, or even a dollar for overshoes. On my milk route I had wet feet, numb feet, and feet with shooting pains. If it hadn't been for the five-minute stop at a grocery hot stove, or a housewife saying, "Poor boy, wouldn't you like to come in and warm yourself?" I would have had a case of bad feet for a long time. I learned a word for what my feet kept singing, "chilblains."

Once I was ten minutes late meeting Mr. Burton where he sat in his wagon in his felt boots. He said, "You're a slowpoke today." I told him, "My feet were near frozen and I had to stop to warm them." He said, "Why don't you get yourself a pair of felt boots like I have?" I said, "We're hard up at our house and I can't spare the two dollars." Mr. Burton sniffed a "humph" as though he couldn't understand what I was saying—which I'm sure he couldn't.

Mr. Burton never sang for himself or me, never joked to me, never told a funny story, never talked about what was in the newspapers or town gossip, never played any kind of music or talked about listening to it, never talked about men or women he liked or funny or mean customers. I wondered sometimes whether George Burton had ever been a boy. What few times I tried to talk with him like I thought a boy could talk with a man, he either cut me off short or he said nothing to me as though I had said nothing to him. But he would stop the horse and wagon for a ten- or fifteen-minute talk with a man in a sulky driving a racehorse. On and on they would talk horse talk.

I came to see that Mr. Burton wasn't ashamed of being a milkman and neither was he proud of it. What he was proud of were two or three horses he had that he hoped to build into a string of horses that would make a name for him. He hoped the milk business might make him enough money to get more horses to breed some world record-breakers. I caught myself saying one day, "He doesn't know boys and if you don't know boys you can't know colts and if you don't know colts you'll never be a big-time horse man."

I got tired of seeing him every day grumpy and frozen-faced, and sometime early in 1893 when he had paid me for my month's work I told him I guessed I didn't want to work for him anymore. He said, "Well, I guess that'll be no loss to me." And I thought of two or three answers I could make but I played a hunch and walked away after saying only "Good-bye, Mr. Burton."

11

In and Out of Jobs

The tinner had his shop on Seminary Street a half block south of Main in a wooden building no bigger than a freight train caboose, with the paint peeling off the boards. A sign in the window read, Tin Work of All Kinds. I had often seen the tinner going in and coming out. He was a medium-small man in clothes that hung loose on him and a slouch hat crumpled on his head. He needed a haircut and hair would stick out from a hole in the hat. I knew he had been in this shop a year or more and that people came to him for tinwork.

I opened the door and walked in one October day to ask if he had a job. He said, without asking whether I had any experience or recommendations or where I last worked, "You can start tomorrow morning at seven." He studied a knothole in the floor half a minute. "I can pay you three dollars a week. Come seven in the morning." He didn't ask my name and I didn't know his.

Next morning I was at the shop at seven. I found the door locked and stood around and waited. Near eight he came along in a one-horse wagon. We loaded an outfit on the wagon and drove out to Broad Street and the house of the well-known Galesburg photographer Osgood. We set up ladders and went up to the low sloping tin roof of the kitchen. I helped him pull loose old and worn tin sheets and carry them to the ladder and down to the ground.

At twelve the boss said we could knock off. I ate a lunch I had brought in a paper bag. It was near two when the boss came back. I hadn't been sure before, but this time I did get a whiff of his whisky breath. He was fumbly going up the ladder. His feet slipped once but his hands kept their hold and he made it to the roof. I followed him with a soldering outfit and made two trips bringing up new sheets of tin. He soldered two or three sheets, and near four said we would knock off for the day.

Next morning I was on hand at seven, and it was nine when my boss came in the wagon, the whisky breath still on him. We drove out to the Osgood house again and he soldered maybe three or four sheets on the roof. At twelve he said we would quit for the day. I was glad because he had slipped again on the ladder and had nearly slid down the roof once. The next morning I was at the shop at eight, waited till ten, walked up and down Main Street a while, came back at eleven and again at twelve to find the door locked.

Then and there I decided I didn't want to learn the tinner's trade. I felt sorry for the tinner and I said, "I won't go back and ask him for my pay— he's too near his finish." A few weeks later I saw the place closed and the sign Tin Work of All Kinds gone.

When I took a job washing bottles in a pop bottling works one summer I knew the future in the job was the same as the past. You washed the same kind of bottles in the morning and afternoon today as you would be washing in the morning and afternoon tomorrow, and yesterday had been the same. You could see the used bottles coming in and the washed bottles going out and it was the same from seven in the morning till six at night. There was one point about the job they told you when they hired you; you could drink all the pop you wanted. I began drinking pop, bottle after bottle. On the fourth day I stopped drinking pop. I had had enough pop to last me a lifetime. At the end of two weeks I quit the job. I didn't like the sight of pop bottles coming in and going out and today the same as yesterday and tomorrow.

There was the late fall and winter I worked in the drugstore of Harvey M. Craig. I had a key and opened the front door at seven in the morning. I swept the floors of the store and prescription room and about half-past seven Mr. Hinman, the pharmacist, came in. I would take a chamois skin and go over the showcases. From the prescription room I took bottles that needed filling and went down in the cellar and turned the spigots of wine barrels and casks of rum and whisky and filled the bottles. There I had my first taste of port wine and claret and found they tasted better than I expected, though I was still leery of what they might do to me. I tasted whisky and decided it was not for me. From the carboys— the champion of all bottles, standing three or four

feet high, and the glass two or three inches thick—
I poured sulphuric acid and muriatic acid, wood
alcohol, turpentine, and other stuff needed upstairs.

At nine o'clock Harvey Craig would come through
the front door and nearly always his wife was with
him. Mr. Craig was a fairly heavy man, though not
big-bodied like his father, Justice A. M. Craig of
the Illinois State Supreme Court. He had something
of his father's face, the mouth stern and the lip ends
pulled down a little. He was kindly with Mr. Hinman
and me, though there was no fun or frolics when he
was around. His wife was small alongside of him
and had quiet and charm. She usually left before
noon.

I liked working with Mr. Hinman. He was slim,
somewhat dark-skinned, with a neat small dark mustache like Edgar Allan Poe. His eyes smiled when
his mouth did. He took an interest in being a pharmacist, had pride about handling drugs and medicines, kept studying the latest finds in medicine.
His sense of humor was always there. He liked to
tell about a boy coming into a drugstore on a hot
summer Sunday and asking for "ten cents' worth of
asafoetida." The clerk climbed up to a shelf and
brought down a bottle, weighed out ten cents' worth,
climbed up and put the bottle back, then climbed
down and wrapped the asafoetida and handed it to

the boy. The boy said, "Charge it." The clerk asked, "What's the name?" "August Schimmelderfer." At which the clerk blurted out, "You little devil, run home with you. I wouldn't spell asafoetida and Schimmelderfer for ten cents!"

In the prescription room was the biggest and thickest book I had ever handled except *Webster's Unabridged Dictionary*. The name was on the front and back covers: *The Pharmacopoeia*. In it were the names of all the drugs there are and what they will do to you. I rambled here and there in it. I asked Mr. Hinman questions about what I read in the book and he was patient and kindly. He liked to share his learning with a younger fellow who had more hopes than he knew what to do with.

For a month or two one winter I took a whirl at the mail-order business. John Sjodin sold me on the idea. He had taken several weekly and monthly papers that were filled with mail-order advertising. He pointed to *Comofort* in Augusta, Maine, with a million subscribers, the biggest circulation of any paper in the country, its columns filled with ads for selling medicines, chickens, kazoos, eyewash, tool kits, knives, music boxes, toys, cheap watches, penny pencils, and more medicines. John said there had been fortunes made in the mail-order business; men

now millionaires had started with just a little printing press. John had bought somewhere for five or
ten dollars a set of type and a tricky little press that
would print a sheet five inches by four. I threw into
the scheme two or three dollars I had saved. I was
the junior partner and would share in the profits the
same percentage as I had put in.

We were going to print a "mail-order journal."
John said, "We will have room in it for advertising
only, so we can't expect to sell it. The subscription
price will be not a cent; so that's what we will name
our mail-order journal." We ran off fifty or sixty
copies, and at the top of the first page was the name
of this new publication in the advertising and selling
field: *Not a Cent*. We followed the first issue with
a second. I forget all that we advertised. But I do
remember we offered for sale one Waterbury watch
"slightly used," a couple of knives "slightly used,"
and we gave the names of several books "slightly
used." We couldn't afford the postage to mail our
"mail-order journal." We gave out here and there
among friends and strangers over half the copies
and kept the rest to look at and say, "We're publishers."

The Sjodin family had moved to the north side
in a working-class neighborhood east of the Q. tracks.
We did our printing in the hayloft of the barn, on

cold days wearing our overcoats and running to the house once in a while to get warm. It was a mile walk across town for me and I ate with John in the Sjodin kitchen. John laughed from beginning to end of this plunge of ours in the mail-order business. Away back in our minds, of course, was a slim glimmering hope—that something would turn up, that a twist of chance might come along and all of a sudden, like it happens every once in a while in a business starting small, we would be on Easy Street. When we quit the business, when *Not a Cent* stopped publication, we laughed the same way as when we first got set for the plunge.

There was the summer I was going to learn the potter's trade. East of Day Street, next to the Peoria tracks, stood a pottery that had been going a year or two. On the ground floor were the turners. You had to be a real potter, who had learned his trade, to be a turner. A turner had a "ball pounder" next to him at the bench. The ball pounder—that was me—weighed on a wooden scale enough clay to make a jug. I would throw this clay on the bench without touching it with my fingers. The fingers wouldn't give the lift needed to carry it in the air and bring it down and cut it in two across a wire. It was a neat trick to learn how to brace your wrists and throw the lower half of the palms of the hands into the clay for this operation. I was warned that my wrists would be sore for a week or two, but after ten days the soreness was over and I could talk to the other ball pounders like I was one of them.

The "ball" you pounded out to a finish was cake-shaped, its size depending on the size of the jug to come. The turner threw it on a turning iron disk, sprinkled water on it, guided it with a hand scraper, and built it up into a jug. Then he stopped the turning disk and slicked out a handle that he smoothed onto the jug. Next, with my hands careful, I moved the jug off the disk and put it on a nearby rack to dry a little before it went for baking to a dome-shaped kiln outside the main building.

On the second floor were the molders, who didn't class up with the turners. They threw the clay into plaster of paris molds on a turning wheel, scraped the inside of the crock or jar, and the mold and the wheel did the rest.

One morning I went down to breakfast to hear that the pottery had burned down in the night. I went out and walked around the smoking walls to see the fire had made a clean sweep of it. It was easy to decide I wouldn't be a potter.

On the main road running past the end of Lake George was a steep hill where the trolley-car motormen put on the brakes going downhill. On the uphill trip it was slow and hard going. So they decided to grade the hill. Men drove mule teams with scrapers, one man driving the mules, another man walking between the handles of the scraper. When the big shovel of the scraper filled up they turned around and dumped it lower down the hill. They went on with this till the hill was a long slope. I was a water boy on this job for three hot summer weeks. I carried two buckets of water from a pump, with two tin cups for each bucket. Some of the men called me "sonny," and it was, "This way, sonny," and "I can stand some of that, sonny," and "You come to the right man, sonny." Then between-times the mules had to have water. I would rather have been water boy just to the men and not to the mules. A mule would often drink nearly a whole pail of water, and it was a hundred yards to the pump.

And one summer I worked for Mr. Winfield Scott Cowan, who ran the boathouse and refreshment stand at Lake George near where the trolley cars stopped. Mr. Cowan had married a daughter of George W. Brown and lived in a big house across the street from the Brown Cornplanter Works. He was a medium-sized man with a dark brown mustache, and he knew how the business should be run, down to such fine points that nearly always he was worrying about this or that not going to come out right. If anything went wrong, he acted as though something else was going to go wrong pretty soon.

My job was to let rowboats to people for twenty-five cents an hour. I would give them the oars, help them pick a boat, and then help them shove off. I had charge of the refreshments and sold ice cream and cake or cookies, pop, ginger ale, and a line of candies.

Mr. Bobbit had charge of the little steamboat that held ten or twelve people, twenty-five cents for a ride to the end of the lake and back. People said she was the prettiest steamboat in Knox County, and as there was no other steamboat in Knox County it was the solemn truth. Her name was *Lady Washington*. Mr. Bobbit kept up steam all day; on some days he had all the passengers he could handle and on other days nobody riding. A man-sized man, Mr. Bobbit, he was tall, broad-shouldered, thick through the body, quick in his motions, and always seemed to know what was going on and what to do. He had a blond mustache and keen eyes that could twinkle. He was English and had been a policeman some-where, I heard. I am sure he was a first-class policeman. He was good company and said, "I worry when it's time to worry and what you don't know sometimes is a help."

It didn't come hard to leave Mr. Winfield Scott Cowan at the end of the season, him and his worrying. Leaving the company of Bobbit wasn't so good. He said he expected a night watchman job in the fall and winter. I said I hoped I'd see him again, though I never did.

Two weeks of ice harvest on Lake George came one January, the thermometer from zero to fifteen above. I walked from home six blocks to catch a streetcar that ran the mile and a half out to the lake. The night gang worked from seven at night till six in the morning, with an hour off at midnight.

The ice was twelve to eighteen inches thick. Men had been over it with horse teams pulling ice cutters. In the first week on the job I was a "floater." Rafts of ice about fifteen feet long and ten feet wide had been cut loose. The floater stood on a raft and, pushing a pronged pole, he propelled the raft and himself to the chutes at the big icehouse. There the ice was broken into blocks or cakes, and a belt carried them up where they were stood in rows with sawdust sprinkled between to hold them cold till summer and warm weather.

I had overshoes and warm clothes and enjoyed the work. The air was crisp, and you could see a fine sky of stars any time you looked up, sometimes a shooting star and films of frost sparkles. I had never had a night job that kept me till the sun came up. I got acquainted with a little of what goes on over the night sky, how the Big Dipper moves, how the spread of the stars early in the night keeps on with slow changes into something else all night long. I did my wondering about that spread of changing stars and how little any one of us is standing and looking up at it.

The other floaters were good fellows and we hollered to each other over the dark water our warnings that if you fell in the water you'd find it cold. At midnight we went up a slope to the Soangetaha Clubhouse of the bon ton. On the porch, away from the windy side, we ate what we had carried out in paper bags.

The second week I was put in the icehouse, where a dozen of us worked on a footing of blocks or cakes of ice, the chute feeding us more cakes of ice. Each cake was about three feet long, two feet wide, and a foot thick. We threw our iron tongs into the end of a cake and then rassled and wrangled it twenty or thirty feet to where it stood even with a row of other cakes. Heavy work, it had my back and shoulder muscles pulling and hauling like a mule. I had never before felt so sure that what I was doing could be done better somehow by mules or machines. I went home the first morning with muscles from ankles to neck sore and aching. I ate breakfast, went to bed right away, and lay abed trying to coax myself to sleep. But muscles would twitch and it was past noon before I went to sleep. Then three or four times I suddenly came awake with the muscles singing. When my mother woke me and said, "It's time to go to work," I was just beginning to sleep, it seemed. I had to unwind myself slowly to get out of bed and into my clothes.

The second night was worse. I would try for a rest by walking slow back to the chute. If I tried for a rest standing still two or three minutes, the foreman would come along, a quiet man saying in a voice that just carried over the noise of the rattling chute and the hustling men, "Better slide into it, Sandburg." If he had bawled or snarled it at me, I would have quit the job on the spot. He remembered my name and I wasn't just a number, I was a person. And he said "Better slide into it" nearly like my mother waking me out of sleep to go to work. I had respect for him and hoped sometime I could be a foreman and act and talk like him.

Near daybreak I thought to myself, "Come seven

o'clock and I'm quitting." I stood still thinking about
it and getting a rest when the foreman came along.
"Better slide into it, Sandburg. You know there's
only a few more days on this job. I think we'll be
through this week." And that gave me a different
feeling. I went home, slept better, ate better, and
the muscles all round weren't as stiff. I lasted the
week through, and at a dollar and twenty-five cents
a night I had earned higher wages than in any work
before. One thing I noticed. I hustled a little too
much. Most of the other men on the job had been
railroad section hands, ditchdiggers, pick-and-shovel
men, and they knew what my father sometimes reminded me of on a piece of work, "Take your time,
Sholly." They worked with a slow and easy swing I
hadn't learned.

I was sixteen or seventeen when I carried water, ran
errands, a few times helped sponge and dry a sweating horse, over six weeks of racing at the Williams
racetrack. What I earned in quarters and half-
dollars ran maybe up to ten dollars. But I had a
pass to come in at any time and I saw up close the
most famous trotting and pacing horses in the world.
    C. W. Williams came to Galesburg from Inde-
pendence, Iowa, where he had what they called a
"kite-shaped" racetrack, though some said it was

more like the figure eight. He had been a telegraph operator and had picked up, at prices that later looked silly, two mares. The world-famous stallions Axtell and Allerton were foaled from those two mares "bought for a song." In 1889 the three-year-old Axtell cut the world's trotting record for stallions down to two minutes and twelve seconds, and on the night of that day was sold to a syndicate for one hundred and fifty thousand dollars, said to be then the highest price ever paid for a horse of any breed. Two years later Mr. Williams could have sold his stallion Allerton for more than he got for Axtell. This was after Mr. Williams himself drove Allerton to cut down the world stallion record to two minutes and nine and three-quarters seconds.

So when Mr. Williams came to Galesburg in 1894 he had a reputation, organized the Galesburg District Association, and laid out a new racetrack on one hundred and twelve acres on the Knoxville Road east of Farnham Street. The new racetrack, Mr. Williams gave it out, was "the only dead-level track in the world." Shaped like a railroad coupling pin, the long sides of it were dead level, with the ends graded for the sulkies to make the turn. In the great six-weeks racing meet that Mr. Williams put on, there were rainy days when races had to be put off and other days when small crowds came, even though the trotters and pacers had national reputations. But there was one big week of good weather and one smashing big day in that week. That was the day we saw the black mare Alix come down the home stretch to break the world's record for trotters.

That day put Galesburg on the map for horsemen and horselovers over the whole country. At the center was Mr. Williams. He was a medium-sized man with an interesting face. He made a great name in the horse world and breeders came from the country over to see him. The blood of his stallions ran for many years in winning horses.

Then harness racing began to run down in style. Mr. Williams sold all his horses for good money and put it into Canada land dealings. I like to think of him as I saw him once on an October morning, a little frost still on the ground, in a sulky jogging around the only dead-level racetrack in the world, driving at a slow trot the stallion Allerton, being kind and easy with Allerton, whose speed was gone but whose seed were proud to call him grandsire.

12

Working for Fun

One night at home we heard the Opera House was
burning and I ran down to the corner of Main and
Prairie to watch it. I stood across the street from the
fire till midnight. I didn't like to see the place go,
I could remember so much about it. There I had
seen the Kickapoo Indians in buckskins and feather
headdress, in dances stomping and howling their
lonesome war songs which we tried to imitate. They

stayed six weeks and I went once or twice a week, admission free. The white man they worked for was a slicker and would put in his spiels: If you had rheumatism or ached in muscles or bones, you eased it with Kickapoo Indian Snake Oil. If you had trouble with stomach or liver you took a few spoons of Kickapoo Indian Sagwa and your insides felt better and a bottle or two cured you. We listened and did imitations of him.

On the stage boards now burning Doctor O'Leary had lectured, admission free. Vegetarianism was his line. What he was selling I forget. He stayed three or four weeks telling what meat does to you, how you have a tired feeling most of the time and you don't have strength for your work. After he left town I didn't eat meat for two weeks, and I found I had the same tired feeling. I began eating meat again and I couldn't feel the poisons so I forgot about Doctor O'Leary.

There on five or six nights one month I had paid my ten cents to sit in the gallery and watch the first mesmerists I had seen. They looked in the eyes of fellows I knew, made passes in front of their faces, and had them fighting bumblebees, or swimming across a carpet. There I saw the body of a living man, his head on one table, his feet on another table, his torso and legs stiff as a hard oak log. A

rock was laid on his body and the powerful blacksmith Ben Holcomb swung a sledge on the rock and
split it. The body stayed stiff and straight through
the whole act. Then the mesmerist snapped his fingers in the fellow's face, said something like "Right!
right!," helped the fellow to his feet, and the two of
them held hands and bowed to the applauding audience. "It wasn't a miracle but it was a wonder,"
we said.

The curving and sizzling tongues of fire licked
away the stage curtain and boards where I had seen
a diorama of the Battle of Gettysburg. They told us
about it at Grammar School, admission five cents.
One diorama curtain after another came down showing different parts of the battle. The curtains were
dirty and worn. The man with a long pointer ex-
plaining the battle had short oily whiskers you couldn't
tell the color of. His clothes looked like he had slept
in them and never brushed them. His voice squeaked.
What he was saying you could tell he had said so
many times that it didn't interest him and his mind
was somewhere else. I was so curious about how
creepy and sad the man with the pointer looked that
half the time I didn't see what he was pointing at.

Before my eyes the boards were burning where
I had first seen Shakespeare's *Hamlet* and was interested only in the killings at the end. I had seen

a man walk out on that stage that I was terribly curious about. I had seen cartoons of him in the Chicago papers, and from what I had read I expected he would tear the air and beat his chest and stamp his enemies under his feet. He was John Peter Altgeld and he was running for governor of Illinois. He just stood in the same foot tracks through his whole speech, about an hour and a half, and never sawed the air once with his hands. The few times he did lift his hands to make a point the motions were as if he could be running a hand along the forehead of a sick friend. He talked in a quiet way as though if we should be quiet too we could make up our minds about what he was saying. I wasn't sure of all he had said but I felt I would be more suspicious of his enemies than of him.

The new Auditorium was built at Broad Street and Ferris and often when out of work and puzzled where to go, I would end up there. It was an up-to-date theater with a main floor, a balcony, and a gallery that was called "Nigger Heaven." The seats nearest to the stage, ten or fifteen rows, were the "parkay." On the tickets it said "parquet." The stage was big enough to handle any show from Broadway, and nearly every Broadway hit heading straight west made a stop at Galesburg.

Some of my work at the Auditorium I got paid for. Mostly I got to see the show for a little work I liked to do. The stage carpenter was American-born of Swedish parents, Oscar Johnson, and everybody called him "Husky." He could drive us and shout at us when there was a rush to be on time with all the scenes and props for the next act, and we took it he had a right to blow off steam. The property man, Charles Rose, everybody called "Cully." He knew he knew everything a property man ought to know and if you wanted an argument he would give it to you. He believed in having props in order and on time. He could do quick headwork and we liked the way he ordered us around. Cully Rose hired the "supes." A supernumerary didn't travel with the show but they had to have their supes. I suped in *McFadden's Flats*. On the stage was an office scene on the eighth floor of a Chicago skyscraper. Offstage four supes watched the man in charge of us. When he went "Ahh-ahh-ahh" real loud and "Ohh-ohh-ohh" louder yet and "Umhh-umhh-umhh" softer, we did the same. What were we doing? We were making the clatter and the rumbling of the Chicago street eight floors below the office on the stage. When the play was showing the big Chicago fire of 1871, the supes ran across the stage with boxes, packages, and bundles, moaning and hollering. Then we ran back around the stage, got different boxes, packages, and bundles, and ran across the stage again trying to give out new moans and yells.

We worked as sceneshifters, and as we finished there might be at our elbows a few steps away a famous star waiting to make her entrance. We would see a comedian in his comic makeup, his face solemn, his eyes on the stage, waiting his cue to go on. A minute later he would be out before the footlights wriggling and twisting, his face and eyes lit up and the audience roaring. Sometimes there would be an actor saying in a low voice the first line he would say when he stepped out on the stage. They brushed by us after their exits, breathing hard after a heavy scene, sometimes limp and sweating.

When we worked in the "flies" we got ten cents a night. We were up thirty or forty feet, and on signals we would send up one curtain and let down another, pulling on ropes. If we got the wrong curtain we certainly heard from down below. Cully Rose could holler and he could be sarcastic. From where we were we could see parts of the play and if there was music or singing we caught it all.

We saw John L. Sullivan closeup playing in *Honest Hearts and Willing Hands*. We could see he liked stepping out on the stage and he wasn't afraid of any audience. In one scene he sat at a table playing he was in trouble and had to use his wits. He put his elbows on the table, dropped his chin into his cupped hands, and then in a whisper he was sure the audience could hear, "Now I must tink." When he took a curtain call he made a fine low bow to the audience, gave a little speech, ended it "I remain yours truly John L. Sullivan," and walked off the stage.

Fridtjof Nansen came. I had read his magazine articles that went into his book *Farthest North*, but I couldn't scrape up the fifty cents to hear him lecture. I was on hand when his train pulled in at the Q. depot, though. It was snowing and I thought he looked like a Scandinavian hero, tall in a long fur coat, as he walked the platform and through the station to where I watched him get into a Union Hotel hack.

When Henry M. Stanley, the African explorer, came to lecture, I was there again at the Q. depot to see him get off the train and tag at his heels through the depot. He wasn't as much to look at as Nansen. To me he was a Famous Writer while Nansen was a Great Norseman and a Viking with a heart for all human strugglers.

James J. Corbett, world's champion boxer, came in *Gentleman Jim*, and his bag-punching opened our eyes. I was following big-league baseball when

I heard that Arlie Latham, the dandy second base-
man of the Cincinnati Reds, would do a song and
dance in a show, and I went to see it. The show
wasn't much and Arlie Latham was no star at singing
and dancing, but I had seen a hero. I didn't see
Bob Fitzsimmons, another world's champion, in his
show. But I did see him on the Q. depot platform,
tall and lanky, with salmon hair and pink skin,
leading a pet lion back and forth.

I helped on the stage when *Monte Cristo* came
to town with James O'Neill the star. The sea that
he swam when he made his escape, the rolling of
that canvas sea, was made by some other boys and
myself. There was the *Uncle Tom's Cabin* show I
peddled bills for and got paid ten cents and a ticket
to the show. The bills said there would be two Uncle
Toms, two Evas, two Simon Legrees, two Elizas
crossing the Ohio River, and two packs of blood-
hounds. We were puzzled how there could be two
of everything, and we went expecting something new
and different. What we saw was just one more Uncle
Tom show, with one of everything instead of two.
The trick brought out a good crowd that would be
suspicious about again paying cash to see two of
everything.

We got used to melodramas where the mortgage
hangs over the house and in the end the villain with

the mortgage gets what is coming to him. Or it might be the will of a dead man and they poked here and there hunting for it, saying "The old will, the old will." Regular on the calendar came a Civil War play with a Union spy in love with a Rebel girl or the other way around, but always wedding bells and appleblossoms in the end. I suped in one of these, *Shenandoah*.

Two famous theater names were Anna Held and John Drew. In cigar stores and saloons a picture hung on the wall showing a woman's hand holding five cards from a deck and the words "This is the hand that Anna Held." And under five cards in a man's hand were the words "This is the hand that John Drew."

If I was on a milk wagon or some other job when minstrels came to town I would manage to have two bits for a ticket to the top gallery. I would try to be on Main Street when the minstrels paraded in tan top hats matching their tan cutaway coats and tan spats, with horns and music in the lead. And when the curtain went up always there would be that Middleman, Mister In-ter-loc-u-tor—on one side six burnt-cork faces over white boiled shirts clicking the rattlebones, on the other side six more with tambourines opening with a song. More than once we heard an End Man ask the Middleman, "Why do the policemen in Monmouth wear rubber boots?" The Middleman couldn't think why in the world the policemen in Monmouth wear rubber boots, and the End Man would reply: "Why, everybody in Monmouth knows the policemen wear rubber boots so as not to wake up the other policemen." We laughed because Galesburg and Monmouth, sixteen miles apart, were jealous of each other and we liked any joke that made Monmouth look silly. We learned that over in Monmouth the minstrels asked why the policemen in Galesburg wore rubber boots! And we giggled at and passed on: "I have pants from Pant-sylvania, a vest from Vest Virginia, a coat from Dacoata, and a hat from Manhattan—am I not an American?"

I missed none of Al Field's minstrel shows. I believed that Al Field was "the undisputed King of the Banjo." When I went to a minstrel show I was satisfied I got my two bits' worth in "Nigger Heaven." You could hear the peanut-eaters cracking the shells, and dropping the shells on the floor. That was expected in the top gallery. On the main floor and in the parquet nobody would dare to be seen eating a peanut. And down there they couldn't yell for a good act nor "mee-ouw" at a bad one.

13

Learning a Trade

They knew at home that I was a helper through the Hard Times, that what I earned counted. They knew I would rather have gone to school. When Mary graduated from high school it was the few dollars I threw in that gave her a nice white dress so she looked as good as any of them on Graduation Day when she stepped out and bowed and took her diploma. We knew that diploma would count. Now she could teach school and be a help and no longer an expense to the family. The next fall she had a country school at thirty dollars a month.

Mary's high school books were a help to me. I didn't study her algebra and Latin textbooks, but I thumbed back and forth in them and got glimmerings. I read Irving's *Sketch Book, Ivanhoe,* and *The Scarlet Letter* and talked with Mary about what the teachers said those novels meant. But the great book Mary brought home—great for what it did to me at that time, opening my eyes about law, government, history, and people—was *Civil Government in the United States* by John Fiske. Here for the first time I read answers to many questions: What are taxes? Who has the taxing power? What is the difference between taxation and robbery? Under what conditions may taxation become robbery? Why does a policeman wear a uniform? What is government? Here I first read the Constitution of the United States and tried to get my head around the English Magna Carta.

There were several months when I read every day in the *Galesburg Evening Mail* the column written in Washington by Walter Wellman. I did a lot of wondering about how one man could know so much about what the government was doing, making plain to millions of people what was going on. From John Fiske's book I learned there are three branches of the government—the executive, the legislative, and the judicial. Walter Wellman made me think I knew what all three branches were doing.

It came over me often that I wasn't getting anywhere in particular. I wanted a job where I could learn a trade. I asked plumbers, carpenters, house painters, and they said there was no opening or I might come around later. When I asked Q. machinists and boilermakers what were the chances they said the Hard Times were still on, old hands waiting to go back. I heard that the Union Hotel barbershop wanted a porter. I said, "Barbering is a trade. A barber can travel, can work in other towns from coast to coast. At barbering you might be shaving a man who'll offer you a job with better money than you can ever make barbering."

I hired to Mr. Humphrey at three dollars a week, plus shoeshine money and tips. The shop was under the Farmers' and Mechanics' Bank, in a half-basement with big windows that let you see the shoes of walkers on the sidewalk. By going up eight steps you could see the Public Square, down Broad Street to the courthouse park, and beyond that the Knox College campus. The floor of the shop was black and white square tiles which I mopped every morning. In rainy weather or snow, with mud tracked in, I gave the floor a once-over again in the afternoon. The big windows to the street I went over once a week with soap and water, sponge and chamois. And the four brass cuspidors had a brisk cleanout every day. Four barber chairs faced a long wall mirror and three times a week I would put a white cleaning fluid on the glass, then with a chamois skin I would wipe off the white stuff.

Mr. Humphrey, Head Barber and Proprietor, had the first chair. At the second chair was a tall fellow with a mustache; his first name John. At the third chair was Frank Wykoff, smooth-faced, with silky golden hair. He had manners and a reputation as a dancer. The fourth chair was worked by Mr. Humphrey's eighteen-year-old son on Saturdays and before holidays when a rush was on.

Of what us kids called "the big bugs on the North Side," many came to the Union Hotel barbershop. "You will meet the bon ton of Galesburg while you work here, Charlie," Mr. Humphrey had said to me. "It's a bluestocking trade comes to our shop and we want to keep the place shipshape, everything clean as a whistle."

Mr. Humphrey was a barber and a gentleman. He would smile and in his pleasant voice say to a regular customer with a nod of the head and a bend of the back and shoulders that was nearly a bow, "Mister Higby, what is the good word with you?" or "Mister Applegreen, how does the world go round for you today?" or "Mister Hagenjos, it's about time we were seeing your good face again." He had a round face with a thin, straight-lined mouth. He was the Boss of the shop and ran it smooth and all had respect for him.

At half-past ten or eleven in the morning, when I saw there would be no customer out of a chair in ten or fifteen minutes, I would go up a back stairs, cross the big main office of the Union Hotel, and go into the most elegant saloon in that part of Illinois. There was a polished mahogany bar, a shining brass rail, tall brass spittoons, a long mirror so those standing at the bar could look at themselves or the other faces at the bar, and wood carving like lace or embroidery on the top and sides of the mirror. Near the end of the bar they set out the free lunch at half-past ten—ham, cheese, pickles, rye and white bread, and sometimes deer or bear meat— and I helped myself. Then I went back to the barbershop thankful to the bartenders for not asking what a minor was doing in the place, and thankful to Solomon Frolich and Henry Gardt, the two German Jews who owned the saloon. I tried to do an extra-special job when I ran my whisk broom over them or gave them a shoeshine.

The Union Hotel got most of the big-time people who came to town, show people, lecturers, minstrels, star actors who had been playing on Broadway and were taking their play from Galesburg to Omaha, to Denver, to Salt Lake City, to San Francisco. Galesburg made a nice one-night stand for them— in the Auditorium across Broad Street from the hotel. In the hotel office, watching people come in and register, I would try to figure out whether they were traveling men or show people. And the pink-sheet *Police Gazette* in the barbershop which I read every week had me on the lookout for the high class confidence men and gamblers who always stopped at high class hotels.

At the desk was James or "Jimmy" Otway, an Englishman who reminded me of people and talk I had met in Dickens' novels. He was short with a blond face, blond hair combed back fancy and wavy, and a thick blond mustache that would have run out far only he kept it well curled, the curliest mustache in town, unless it was Will Olson's. He wore light tweed suits, stiff stand-up collars and stiff starched cuffs, colored neckties, and was spick-and-span. He bred blooded beagles and there might be two or three of his brown-and-white-haired dogs running around the office. Jimmy Otway belonged to the town and you were not quite a Galesburger unless you knew about him. I waited around sometimes to see whether he would drop his "aitches" and I learned there are Englishmen who don't drop their "aitches."

On my seventeenth birthday, January 6, 1895, General Philip Sidney Post died. He had served five terms as Congressman from our district, and was beginning his sixth when he died. Senators and Congressmen, old soldiers of the Civil War, politicians from far and near, came to his funeral. At the Q. depot I watched a noon train from Chicago pull in with a special car loaded with men wearing Prinz Albert coats and high silk hats. Then I walked to the Union Hotel barbershop to find every barber chair filled and a line of customers wearing Prinz Albert coats in the waiting chairs. The hatrack was filled with silk hats, and more of the same shiny hats were in a row on two window ledges.

I took to my shoeshine stand, where already the first customer was waiting. I shined the shoes of four Senators, eight Congressmen, two or three majors, and two pairs of knee-high boots of the same kind Lincoln wore. It was my banner day as a shoeshine boy. Most of them handed me the regular nickel pay. Some gave me a dime and two whose breath told me they could have been at the Union Hotel bar dropped a quarter into the hand I held out. For the first time I earned $1.40 in one day.

When I had seen Philip Sidney Post on the streets, I didn't think of him as any special hero. He was a man of stocky build, thick through the body, with a round head and face and a straight nose. He was a little bald over the forehead and had a longish dark mustache and a little goatee you had to look twice to see. Later I learned that Post was a great fighting man, one of the best soldiers who answered Lincoln's call for troops in '61. He was a young lawyer out in Wyandotte, Kansas, when the call came. He went east to Galesburg, enlisted, became second lieutenant of Company A, 59th Illinois Volunteer Infantry, and fought in some of the bloodiest battles of the war, taking wounds, getting honorable mentions, moving up to major, colonel, and brigadier general. Pea Ridge, Perryville, Murfreesboro, Chickamauga were bloody grounds, and Post was there. After the war his corps commander, General George H. Thomas, asked the Secretary of War to make him a colonel in the regular army.

Post had come back to Galesburg in 1879 after serving thirteen years as consul and then consul-general at Vienna, and he went into the real estate business. One day General Post with two other men came into the Union Hotel barbershop. All three had shaves and two had shines. One of the two whose shoes I shined was Philip Sidney Post. If I had known where those feet had been in their time I would have tried to turn out the best and brightest shine I ever put on shoe leather.

In the barbershop on Saturday I was here, there, and everywhere. Next to the shop was a bathroom with eight tubs and partitions between, twenty-five cents for a bath. For those who asked it I would get a tub of hot water ready. There were two or three regulars who would call me in to scrub their backs with a brush. Nearly always those I gave special help to paid me a quarter.

The worst mistake I made was one they guyed me about for a long time. The gentleman had had a shave, a haircut, and a shampoo. I gave him a shoeshine. He looked good for a dime tip, at least a nickel. I swung my whisk broom over his Prinz Albert coat and his pants down to the shoes. Then I took his high silk hat off the hatrack. I began swinging my whisk broom up, down, and around his hat, the first hat of the kind I had ever handled. He had finished paying his bill to Mr. Humphrey when he looked over to where I was. He let out a howl and rushed over yelling, "You can't do that!" I saw at once what he meant; I had been an ignoramus about silk hats. I tried to mumble something about being sorry. I saw the two barbers trying to keep from laughing. Mr. Humphrey came up and I heard him say the only sharp words he ever said to me, ending up with talking natural, "Charlie, you ought to have a soft brush for silk hats or a satin cloth." The customer had snatched his hat out of my hands and held it as though I might of a sudden jump at him and tear the hat away. He handed me a nickel for the shine and walked out as though he certainly would never come back to this place. The next day I had a soft satin cloth on hand and a brush with hairs so soft you could hardly feel them running over the palm of your hand. And after that when once in a while a silk hat came into the shop I was ready for it. I had what they call "confidence" because I had been through what they call "experience."

The barbers, among themselves as barbers, talked about razors. Most of them swore by the Wade & Butcher razor. It interested me that there was a razormaker whose name was Butcher. A fellow with a tough and tangled beard they called a "squirrel." One of them had just gone out the door when Frank Wykoff, who had shaved him, was saying, "He was a squirrel, all right. After I started on him I knew

I had to lather him again and rub it in deep. I stropped my razor six times. You can't cut his whiskers. You have to whittle 'em."

Two or three times a week I would meet two other boys who were portering in barbershops. We talked about what blacking was best for a shoe, the rougher shoes that need two coats of blacking before you put on the brushes, and how to look at a customer or what to say that would make him think it would be a good idea to pay you a dime instead of a nickel. One of these boys, Harry Wade, thought he had a sidewise look up into the customer's face, along with a smile, that sometimes brought him an extra nickel. The other homely porter and I said to Harry, "You're a good-looker and wear smart clothes and that's more than half of why you get more tips than we do." Harry might not like the looks of a customer and after he gave him a brush-off that had everything, if he got no tip, he could say "Thank you" with a sarcastic sneer. The Head Barber caught on to this and said, "You're a good porter, Harry, but if you keep that up, we'll have to let you go."

Harry and the other porters used to dress in their fanciest clothes and Sunday noon walk into the Brown's Hotel dining room and order a fifty-cent dinner. They called it "classy." Their home folks set a good table, but after being barbershop porters all week they wanted to "sit with the bon ton." Harry Wade had the only snare drum in our neighborhood. He brought it to the Berrien Street pasture, where at night the boys sat on the grass while he stood and gave us all the drum taps he knew. Harry's arms and wrists were fast with the sticks; he practiced hard and hoped to get on with a band and travel. Every one of us wished he had a classy snare drum and was good with the sticks like Harry. He had class enough without eating fifty-cent dinners at Brown's Hotel on Sundays.

Harry came along one night in 1893 to where we were sitting in the pasture. He had just got off a train from Chicago, where he had had three days at the World's Fair, the great Columbian Exposition. He sat down with us and talked for an hour about the fair. When he quit talking we put questions to him and he went on talking and gave us the feel of that World's Fair up in Chicago. We couldn't afford to go and Harry brought parts of it to us.

Spring came after fall and winter months in the barbershop and doubts had been growing in me that I wasn't cut out for a barber. Spring moved in with smells on the air, and Sam Barlow came into my life. He had sold his farm up near Galva and gone into the milk business. He was a jolly, laughing man, short, tough-muscled, a little stoop-shouldered, with a ruddy, well-weathered face, brown eyes, a thick sandy mustache, and a voice I liked. He had been a barn-dance fiddler, and still liked to play.

Barlow stopped his milk wagon one day, called me from a sidewalk, and asked if I wanted to go to work for him at twelve dollars a month and dinner with him and his wife every day. I took him up on it. It would be outdoor work; I would see plenty of sky every day. The barbershop had been getting stuffy. I parted from Mr. Humphrey and it wasn't easy to tell him, "You've been fine to me, Mr. Humphrey, but I've got to be leaving. I don't think I'm cut out for a barber."

14

A Milk Route Again

Every morning for sixteen months or more I walked from home at half-past six, west on Berrien Street, crossing the Q. switchyard tracks, on past Mike O'Connor's cheap livery stable, past the Boyer broom factory, then across the Knox College campus and past the front of the Old Main building. Every morning I saw the east front of Old Main where they had put up the platform for Lincoln and Douglas to debate in October 1858. At the north front of Old Main many times I read on a bronze plate words spoken by Lincoln and by Douglas. They stayed with me, and sometimes I would stop to read those words only, what Lincoln said to twenty thousand people on a cold windy October day: "He is blowing out the moral lights around us, when he contends that whoever wants slaves has a right to hold them." I read them in winter sunrise, in broad summer daylight, in falling snow or rain, in all the weathers of a year.

Then I continued along South Street to Monmouth Boulevard to the house and barn of Samuel Kossuth Barlow. There I shook out straw and shoveled clean the stalls of three horses, sometimes packed mud into the sore foot of a horse, hitched a horse to a wagon. By that time Bill Walters, a good-looking husky with a brown mustache, would have come in from two farms west of town, bringing the day's milk to be delivered. Mr. Barlow would be out of the house, and Harry ("Fatty") Hart would show up. He wasn't fat but the boys had hung the nickname of "Fatty" on him and it stuck. He was straight and square-shouldered, with round cheeks maybe puffed out a little, and black hair, black eyes, and a bright quick smile. While Bill Walters went with his wagon and worked to the north, Mr. Barlow and Fatty and I covered the south side of town.

Sam Barlow was different from George Burton. He would take a two-gallon can of milk and walk a route of a few blocks while Fatty or I drove the wagon. He would keep telling us to pay respect to any complaints of customers, never to "sass" them, whereas Burton used to act as though it was something special for people to get their milk from him. Mr. Barlow had us keep an eye out for any house people were moving out of, and when new people came in we would be on the spot asking if they wouldn't like to have milk from us. Usually we got a new customer. From October on, when the cows didn't have pasture, we sold eighteen quart tickets for a dollar; then in summer twenty for a dollar. Starting in early June, till about the middle of September, we made two deliveries a day. Most customers didn't have iceboxes and didn't want their milk to sour overnight. That meant Mr. Barlow and I would wash all the cans twice a day in the warm-weather months—the big eight-gallon cans that stayed on the wagon and the two- and three-gallon cans we carried and poured out the pints and quarts from. After washing up we always had a good dinner set out by Mrs. Barlow and her daughter.

To one house every day I carried a small can

holding the milk of one cow. A doctor had ordered the baby in that house to have milk from one cow and every day the same cow. We were proud to be doing this because the father of the baby was Frank Bullard, whose name had been flashed to newspapers all over the country as the engineer on a fast mail train that set a new world's record for locomotive and train speed. I would see him walk out of his house and up the street carrying a wicker lunchbox, walking cool and taking it easy—a square-shouldered, upstanding man with black hair and a black mustache. We did the best we could to see that the baby never changed cows. But there were two or three times we couldn't help it; milk and cans got mixed up and the baby got the milk of several cows, and we never heard but the baby was doing well.

It was on my milk route that I had my "puppy love." Day and night her face would be floating in my mind. Her folks lived on Academy Street next to the Burlington tracks of the Q. They usually left a crock on the porch with a quart ticket in it. I would take the ticket out of the crock, tilt my can and pour milk into my quart measure, then pour it into the crock, well aware she was sometimes at the kitchen window watching my performance, ducking away if

I looked toward the window. Two or three times a week, however, the crock wasn't there and I would call "Milk!" and she would come out with the crock in her hands and a smile on her face. At first she would merely say "Quart" and I would pour the quart and walk away. But I learned that if I spoke a smooth and pleasant "Good morning," she would speak me a "Good morning" that was like a blessing to be remembered. I learned too that if I could stumble out the words, "It's a nice day" or "It's a cold wind blowing" she would say a pert "Yes, it is" and I would go away wondering how I would ever get around to a one- or two-minute conversation with her.

It was a lost love from the start. It began to glimmer away after my first and only walk with her. I dropped in with another boy one summer night to revival services at the Knox Street Congregational Church. There I saw her with another girl. After the services my chum took the other girl and I found myself walking with the girl of my dreams. I had said, "See you home?" and she had said, "Certainly." And there we were walking in a moonlight summer night and it was fourteen blocks to her home. I said it was a mighty fine moonlight night. She said "Yes" and we walked a block saying nothing. I said it was quite a spell of hot weather we had been having. She said "Yes" and we walked another block. I said one of the solo singers at the church did pretty good. Again she agreed and we walked on without a word. I spoke of loose boards in the wooden sidewalk of the next block and how we would watch our step.

I had my right hand holding her left arm just above the elbow, which I had heard and seen was the proper way to take a girl home. And my arm got bashful. For blocks I believed maybe she didn't like the way I was holding her arm. After a few blocks it was like I had a sore wooden arm that I ought to take away and have some peace. Yet I held on. If I let go I would have to explain and I couldn't think of an explanation. I could have broken one of the blocks we walked without a word by saying, "Would you believe it, your face keeps coming back to me when I'm away from you—all the time it keeps coming back as the most wonderful face my eyes ever met." Instead I asked her how her father, who was a freight train conductor on the Q., like being a conductor.

The fourteen blocks came to an end. At her gate I let go of her arm, said "Good night," and walked away fast, as if I had an errand. I didn't even stand to see if she made it to the front door. I had made the decision that we were not "cut out for each other." I had one satisfaction as I walked home. My bashful right arm gradually became less wooden.

After sixteen or eighteen months with Barlow, at twelve dollars a month and a good dinner every day, I asked him for a raise. He said the business couldn't stand it. I had to say, "I hate to leave you. You're the best man I ever worked for but I can't see I'm getting anywhere." He said, "If you have to go, then all right, Charlie. What has to be has to be. You've been a good boy and we've had some good times together. I hope you'll come around and see us once in a while." And I did. They put in a new Edison phonograph with a lot of cylinder records and I never got tired of hearing "Poet and Peasant." Sam Barlow and I stayed good friends as long as he lived.

15

On the Road

I had my bitter and lonely hours moving out of boy years into a grown young man. But I had been moving too in a slow way to see that to all the best men and women I had known in my life and especially all the great ones I had read about, life wasn't easy, life had often its bitter and lonely hours, and when you grow with new strengths of body and mind it is by struggle. I was through with *Tom the Bootblack, From Rags to Riches,* and the books by Horatio Alger. Every one of his heroes had a streak of luck. There was a runaway horse and the hero saved a rich man's daughter by risking *his* life to grab the reins and save *her* life. He married the daughter and from then on life was peaches and cream for him.

There was such a thing as luck in life but if luck didn't come your way it was up to you to step into struggle and like it. I read Ouida's *Under Two Flags.* The hero lost everything he had except a horse, lived a dirty and bloody life as a fighting man, with never a whimper. I read Olive Schreiner's *The Story of an African Farm,* sad lives on nearly every page, and yet a low music of singing stars and love too deep ever to be lost. I believed there were lives far more bitter and lonely than mine and they had fixed stars, dreams and moonsheens, hopes and mysteries, worth looking at during their struggles. I was groping.

I was nineteen years old, nearly a grown man. And I was restless. The jobs I'd had all seemed deadend with no future that called to me. Among the boys I could hold my own. With the girls I was bashful and couldn't think of what to say till after I left them, and then I wasn't sure. I had never found a "steady."

I read about the Spanish General Weyler and his cruelties with the people of Cuba who wanted independence and a republic. I read about Gomez, Garcia, Maceo, with their scrabbling little armies fighting against Weyler. They became heroes to me. I tried to figure a way to get down there and join one of those armies. I would have signed up with any recruiting agent who could have got me there. Nothing came of this hope.

What came over me in those years 1896 and 1897 wouldn't be easy to tell. I hated my hometown and yet I loved it. And I hated and loved myself about the same as I did the town and the people. I came to see that my trouble was inside of myself more than it was in the town and the people.

I decided in June of 1897 to head west and work in the Kansas wheat harvest. I would beat my way on the railroads; I would be a hobo and a "gaycat." I had talked with hoboes enough to know there is the professional tramp who never works and the gaycat who hunts work and hopes to go on and get a job that suits him. I would take my chances on breaking away from my hometown where I knew every street and people in every block and farmers on every edge of town.

I had never been very far from Galesburg. I was sixteen when for the first time I rode a railroad train for fifty miles. I opened a little bank of dimes and found I had eighty cents. My father got me a pass on the Q. and I rode alone to Peoria and felt important and independent. I saw the State Fair and sat a long time looking at the Illinois River and the steamboats. I was a traveler seeing the world, and when I got home I couldn't help telling other people how Peoria looked to me.

I had made my first trip to Chicago only the year before, when I was eighteen. I had laid away one dollar and fifty cents and my father, after years of my begging for it, got me a pass on the Q. I was traveling light, no valise or bag. In my pockets I had my money, a knife, a piece of string, a pipe and tobacco and two handkerchiefs. John Sjodin had coached me how to live cheap in Chicago. The longer my dollar and a half lasted, the longer I could stay. I ate mostly at Pittsburgh Joe's on Van Buren near Clark Street, breakfast a high stack of wheat pancakes with molasses and oleo and coffee with a dash of milk in it, all for five cents. Dinner was a large bowl of meat stew, all the bread you wanted, and coffee, at ten cents. Supper was the same.

A room on the third floor of a hotel on South State Street was twenty-five cents a night. The rickety iron bedstead with its used sheets took up most of the bare wooden floor space. In the corners were huddles of dust and burnt matches. There were nails to hang my clothes on, and I went down a dark narrow hallway to a water closet and washroom with a roller towel.

I went two nights to the Variety Show, vaudeville, in a top gallery at ten cents. I mustn't miss at ten cents the Eden Musée on South State, John Sjodin had said, and there I saw in wax Jesse James and several murderers. I walked through the big State Street department stores I had heard about for years, Siegel Cooper's at Van Buren and north to Marshall Field's. I stood in front of the Daily News Building, the Tribune and Inter-Ocean buildings. I had carried and sold so many of their papers that I wanted to see where they were made. I had great respect for Victor Lawson and his *Record* and *Daily News* and I would have liked to go into his office and speak to him but I couldn't think of what I would say.

I walked miles and never got tired of the roar of the streets, the trolley cars, the teamsters, the drays, buggies, surreys, and phaetons, the delivery wagons high with boxes, the brewery wagons piled with barrels, the one-horse and two-horse hacks, sometimes a buckboard, sometimes a barouche with a coachman in livery, now and again a man in a saddle on horseback weaving his way through the traffic—horses, everywhere horses and here and there mules—and the cobblestone streets with layers of dust and horse droppings. I walked along Michigan Avenue and looked for hours to where for the first time in my life I saw shimmering water meet the sky. I walked around every block in the Loop, watched the frameworks of the Elevated lines shake and tremble and half expected a train to tumble down to the street. I dropped in at the Board of Trade and watched the grain gamblers throwing fingers and yelling prices.

The afternoon of my third day in Chicago I stopped in at a saloon with a free-lunch sign. I helped myself to slices of rye bread and hunks of cheese and baloney, paid a nickel for a glass of beer. I didn't care much for beer but I had heard so much about Chicago saloons that I wasn't going to leave without seeing the inside of one.

I had seen Chicago for three days on a dollar and a half. I rode home and tried to tell the folks what Chicago was like. None of them had ever been there except Papa and Mama and they had stayed only long enough to change trains. I was glad to be back in a room with a clean floor and a bed with clean sheets and it was good to have Mama's cooking after Pittsburgh Joe's. Yet there were times I wished I could be again in those street crowds and the roaring traffic.

Now I would take to The Road. The family didn't like the idea. Papa scowled. Mama kissed me and her eyes had tears after dinner one noon when I walked out of the house with my hands free, no bag or bundle, wearing a black-sateen shirt, coat, vest, and pants, a slouch hat, good shoes and socks, no underwear. In my pockets were a small bar of soap, a razor, a comb, a pocket mirror, two handkerchiefs, a piece of string, needles and thread, a Waterbury watch, a knife, a pipe and a sack of tobacco, three dollars and twenty-five cents.

It was the last week in June, an afternoon bright and cool. A little west of the Santa Fe station stood a freight train waiting for orders. As the train started I ran along and jumped into a boxcar. I stood at the open side door and watched the running miles of young corn. Crossing the long bridge over the Mississippi my eyes swept over it with a sharp hunger that the grand old river satisfied. Except for my father, when riding to Kansas to buy land, no one of our family had seen the Father of Waters. As the train slowed down in Fort Madison, I jumped out.

I bought a nickel's worth of cheese and crackers

and sat eating and looking across the Mississippi. The captain of a small steamboat said I could work passage to Keokuk unloading kegs of nails. I slept on the boat, had breakfast, sailed down the river watching fields and towns go by—at Burlington, Quincy, and Keokuk shouldering kegs of nails to the wharves. At Keokuk I spread newspaper on green grass near a canal and slept in the open. I washed my face and hands at the canal, using soap from my pocket and drying with a handkerchief. Then I met a fellow who said, "On the road?" When I said "Yes," he led me to where he had been eating bread and meat unwrapped from a newspaper. "I got three lumps last night," he said, and handed me a lump. A lump was what you were handed if you got something to eat at a house where you asked for it. My new friend said, "I got a sitdown before I got the lumps." At one house he had been asked to sit at the kitchen table and eat. Then because he wanted to have this day free to look at the canal and the blue sky, he went from house to house for lumps, hiding them under wooden sidewalks so his hands were empty. The lump he gave me had four slices of buttered bread and two thick cuts of roast beef. "This is breakfast and dinner for me," I said.

His face and hands were pudgy as though your fingers would sink into them if you touched them.

He had come out of a Brooklyn orphan asylum, had taken to The Road, and said he had never done a day's work in his life. He was proud he had found a way to live without working. He named Cincinnati Slim and Chicago Red and other professional tramps he had traveled with, as though they were big names known to all tramps and I must have heard of them. He named towns where the jail food was good and how in winter he would get a two or three months' sentence for vagrancy in those jails. "Or I might go South for the cold weather," he said, "keeping away from the towns where they're horstyle." Now I had learned that where they are hostile they are "hor-style" in tramp talk. He had a slick tongue and a fast way of talking, and soon I walked away, leaving him where he lay on the green grass looking at the blue sky. I would have felt sorry for him if he wasn't so sure he could take care of himself.

During a heavy rainstorm that night I slept in the dry cellar of a house the carpenters hadn't finished and I was up and out before they came to work. I had a fifteen-cent breakfast, found an old tomato can, bought a cheap brush, and had the can filled with asphaltum for a few nickels. Then I went from house to house in several blocks and got three jobs blacking stoves that were rusty, earning seventy-five cents, and two jobs where my pay was dinner and supper. I slept again in the house the carpenters hadn't finished and the next day went from house to house and got no jobs with pay brushing alphaltum on rusty stoves, though I did get breakfast, dinner, and supper for three jobs. The day after I bought a refill of asphaltum, earned three meals and twenty-five cents. The following day was the same as the day before. I found that the housewives were much like those for whom I had poured milk in Galesburg. I found, too, that if I said I was hoping to earn money to go to college they were ready to help me. The trouble was there were not enough rusty stoves.

The next day was the Fourth of July, with crowds pouring into Keokuk. I saw a sign "Waiter Wanted" in a small lunch counter near the end of Main Street. The owner was running the place by himself and said I could make myself useful at fifty cents a day and meals. He showed me the eggs, lard, and frying pan, the buns and ham for sandwiches, the doughnuts and the coffeepot. At ten o'clock he went out, telling me I was in charge and to be polite serving customers. Three or four people drifted in before eleven-thirty, when he came back, feeling good, he said, and he would help through the noon rush. Five or six customers came in the next two hours and he sat in a quiet corner taking a sleep while I handled the trade. There were not more than two customers at any one time and I flourished around, got them what they called for on our plain and simple bill of fare. I felt important. Maybe after a while I might work up to be a partner in the business.

The owner woke up and went out saying he would be back soon. At three o'clock he came in feeling better than the last time. He had forgotten to eat at noon and I offered to fix him two fried eggs, which I served him with a bun and coffee. He went out again saying he would be back soon. At five o'clock he came back "stewed to the gills," slumped himself in a corner on the floor, and went to sleep. I fried myself three eggs and ate them with two buns and coffee. I fixed two sandwiches with thick cuts of ham, put them in my coat pockets along with two doughnuts, opened the money drawer and took out a half-dollar. With my coat on one arm, I closed the front door softly, and that night slept in a boxcar that took me halfway across the State of Missouri. For a poor boy seeking his fortune I hadn't done so bad for one day.

Next was the railroad section gang at Bean Lake, Missouri. My Irish boss, Fay Connors, hired me at a dollar and twenty-five cents a day and I was to pay him three dollars a week for board and room in his four-room one-story house thirty feet from the railroad tracks. There were five of us in the gang and you would have known Connors was the boss. He liked his voice and his authority. At no time did he get mad and bawl out a man, but he had a frozen-faced way of letting men know he was once a section *hand* and was now a section *boss*. I tamped ties several days from seven till noon and from one till six. My muscles ached at night like they did when I worked in the ice harvest. Then came weed cutting. We swung our scythes along the right of way; I had to train a new set of muscles and *they* ached at night.

At morning, noon, and evening, the meals at the Connors table were the same, fried side pork, fried potatoes, and coffee. Connors seemed to like it. So did his wife and three small children. At the end of two weeks, on a Sunday morning, I hopped a freight for Kansas City and left Boss Connors to collect for my board and room out of my paycheck.

In Kansas City Mrs. Mullin had a sign in the window of her restaurant on Armour Avenue, "Dishwasher Wanted." She took the sign out when the Swede boy from Illinois made himself at home in the kitchen. Noontime was the rush hour of the workers from the meat-packing plants nearby. It was a fight in that dish trough to get enough dishes cleaned for serving the customers. I swept the eating room morning and afternoon and mopped it on Saturday. My sleeping place was the end of a hallway with my cot curtained off, and I washed and shaved, using my pocket mirror, at a sink in the hall.

I was up at six in the morning and had the eating room swept for customers who began coming at six-thirty when we opened. I worked every weekday till eight at night except for an hour or two in the afternoon. I had good times in that kitchen. The mulatto chef was fat, jolly, always cheerful and would fix me three good meals a day. He would ask what I wanted as though he was an uncle of mine and nothing was too good for me. The one waiter was also a mulatto. George was handsome and gay, could sing either oldtime songs or late hits, and would sing special songs I called for. I had Sunday off and walked miles around Kansas City.

In a week or so the wheat harvest in western Kansas would be ready. Mrs. Mullin paid me my second week's pay of one dollar and fifty cents and I said good-bye and saw the sign "Dishwasher Wanted" whisked back into the window. Saying good-bye to George and the chef wasn't easy. They were good-hearted men who had made everything easier and brighter for me.

I slept two nights in a fifteen-cent second-floor "flophouse" where forty men in one room each had a cot about an arm's length apart. A near neighbor might be snoring, and at two or three in the morning there might be a scream from a fellow waking out of a bad dream. Worst of all were the flat brown creepers who could bite into your skin so you were awake on the instant. They had homes in our blankets. We had no sheets.

Hopping freight trains on my way west I had one bad afternoon. A shack (hobo for brakeman) had ordered me off an open coal car where I was crouched. When the train started I got on again. The train was running full speed when he climbed down from the car ahead and another shack followed him. He put his face close to mine. "I told you to stay off this train. Now you'll come through with two bits or you'll take what you get." It was my first time with a shack of that kind. I had met brakemen who were not small-time grafters, and one who spotted me in a boxcar corner said, "If you're going to ride, keep out of sight." I figured I might owe the railroad money for fare but the shack wasn't a passenger-fare collector. So I didn't come through with two bits. He outweighed me by about forty pounds and when his right fist landed on my left jaw and his left fist slammed into my mouth I went to the floor. As I slowly sat up, he snarled, "Stay where you are or you'll get more." Then as he and his partner turned to go he gave me a last look and laughed, "You can ride, you've earned it."

I stood up and watched the passing land. The trees were few, no such timber as in Illinois and Missouri. I had come to the Great Plains. I was traveling, though my handkerchief was splotched red from putting it to my mouth. When the train slowed down I got off and found myself at a hobo jungle, two men leaving to catch the train I had quit, two more washing their shirts in a shallow creek shaded by three cottonwood trees. I washed my shirt, socks, and handkerchief. The two men were gaycats, said they had spent their last nickel for a loaf of bread and a half-pound of Java and could I scrape the nickels for a few weenies? I said fair enough and went for the weenies and we ate well. I caught a freight that night that had me in Emporia, where I walked past the office of the *Emporia Gazette* but didn't have the nerve to step in and see the editor, William Allen White. After a big two-bit meal I went to the city park where I lay on the grass for a sleep and then talked with two men who got me to singing for them. They were professional tramps and wanted me to go along with them. They were sure I could make money singing in saloons, and they had the idea we would all share in the money so made. It seemed a little queer to me.

That night a bright full moon was up in a clear sky and out past the Sante Fe water tank waiting their chances to catch a freight train west was a gay bunch of eight men, most of them heading toward the wheat harvest. In a windy rain I jumped out of the boxcar I caught in Emporia and found a sleeping place under a loading platform for stock cars. About seven in the morning I read the station sign and learned I was in Hutchinson, Kansas. I had heard it was better not to hit the houses near the railroad; they had been hit too often by 'boes. I walked eight or ten blocks and hit two houses. "Have you got any work I can do for breakfast?" At each they took one look at me and shut the door. At the third house a woman sent her daughter to get me a saw, showed me a woodpile and a sawbuck. For an hour I kept the saw going, piled the wood, and went to the house. The smiling mother and daughter led me to the family table, set fried ham and potatoes, applesauce, bread and coffee, before me. After I had eaten they handed me a large lump. I thanked them, walked Main Street to see what Hutchinson was like, and went to my loading platform. Unwrapping the lump, I found fried chicken and bread that would make dinner and supper, along with two pocketsful of apples that had come down in the wind and rain the night before.

Lindsborg, Kansas, was Swedish, and Pastor Swenson, the head of Bethany College there, was a

Lutheran Synod leader I had heard preach in Galesburg. It was either hay or broomcorn harvest I worked in with other Swedes on a farm near Lindsborg. I stayed three days at a dollar a day and meals, sleeping in a barn hayloft. On my third and last morning I had been awake a few minutes when I heard voices down below. One voice came clear, a Swede saying, "Is that bum up yet?" I said to myself, "Am I a bum?" And I had to answer, "Yes, I am a bum." I had bummed my way to Lindsborg; I had no baggage nor bundle and I expected to bum my way on a train out of Lindsborg. The first time in my life I heard myself referred to as a bum was among Swedes I had made a detour to see. I was getting no such hand of fellowship as from George and the chef in the Kansas City kitchen.

Newspapers said the country was pulling out of the Hard Times, yet there were many men still out of work, men who had left their homes hoping for jobs somewhere, riding the boxcars and sitting around the jungle hangouts. Some had learned hobo slang; some didn't care for it. There was always a small fraternity who knew each other at once by their slang. They were the professional tramps, who divided into panhandlers and petty thieves. Panhandlers talked about "how to work Main Street," what kind of faces to ask for a dime or a quarter. "Never mooch a goof wearing a red necktie," I heard. They would argue about the best kind of story to melt the heart of the citizen you walked along with. The longer you made your story, the more danger there was that the citizen would ask you questions and maybe while you were answering a cop would come along "and he sees you're a vag and jugs you." "I think I'll try the goat in this town," said one and I learned the goat was the Catholic priest. "I had a good snooze in a knowledge box last night," meant the fellow had slept in a country schoolhouse.

The petty thieves did less talking. The only one who got confidential with me wore a good brown suit, a brown shirt with a brown necktie. His face and mustache were like the pictures of the hero in the *Family Story Paper*. His quiet words to me were, "I'm a second-story man. I could use you." He would have me stand on his shoulders and climb up on a porch, go through a window, and search for money and jewels we would split. He hadn't been doing so well lately but he had seen good times and they would come again. He had a soft voice and he was polite. I told him I would think about it, but I managed to get away from him without telling him what I thought about it.

I was meeting fellow travelers and fellow Americans. What they were doing to my heart and mind, my personality, I couldn't say then nor later and be certain. I was getting a deeper self-respect than I had had in Galesburg, so much I knew. I was getting to be a better storyteller. You can be loose and easy when from day to day you meet strangers you will know only an hour or a day or two. What girls I was meeting on a job or at a sitdown usually wanted to know where I was from, where I was going, what kind of a home and folks I had, and I was working out of my bashfulness.

On one boxcar ride there was a young farmhand from Indiana I liked so much that I asked him how it would be for the two of us to travel together and share and share alike for a few weeks. He said he would shake hands on it if I would go with him to the Klondike. The gold rush was on and he was heading for Alaska. He had expected to stop for the Kansas wheat harvest and earn money he needed but now he figured that might make him a little late in getting to the Chilkoot Pass and the gold waiting for the early ones. We were sorry to part.

At Larned, Pawnee County, Kansas, I refused to regard myself as a hobo. My father had owned land in that county and had set foot in this town when he came to look at the land. I had written for my father the letters sending tax payments to the Country Treasurer of Pawnee County. When I walked past the courthouse I felt like an important, respectable citizen. You could walk the few blocks of Main Street in about three minutes. You could see empty houses here and there; people had moved away because of Hard Times. The weekly paper was worth reading if only for its name, the *Tillers and Toilers Journal.*

For three days I worked at seventy-five cents a day helping a carpenter. I worked five days with a crew threshing wheat—three days on one farm and two days on another—pitchforking bundles of wheat onto the tables of the thresher. It was hard work but the crew was jolly, the meals good, the barns clean where four of us slept on hay, the pay a dollar and twenty-five cents a day and board. Then there was to be no more work till five days later. I decided to head west to Lakin, where I heard there was more doing.

In the days between work I had long talks and shared meals at the Santa Fe water tank with an odd bird from Kansas City. He said he had been a bookkeeper for a coal firm there several years. They had let him out because business was slow. He seemed to have money and he had a six-shooter that he took out once in a while and fingered. He had an interesting face with a hawk nose, a good mouth, and a chin that pointed out. His blue eyes had some kind of danger that I couldn't make out. He was friendly with me and seemed to hint that maybe we could travel together.

But I went on alone to Lakin, which I noticed on a timetable was six hundred and eighty-four miles from Galesburg on the Santa Fe. I figured that with detours I had traveled a thousand miles since I left home. I worked with a threshing crew some three weeks around Lakin. The job finished on one farm, we moved to another farm with a different farmer and family.

A shack put me off the bumpers of a fast freight I had caught out of Lakin. A minute after I got off, I ran into the blue-eyed bird from Larned. It was near midnight. We went to a lunch counter and he insisted on paying. He had a roll of bills, and he said, "I'm flush." I told him I was catching the next freight out if there was an empty boxcar I could sleep in. He walked with me to the water tank, where he pulled the revolver from his hip pocket, saying, "This gat comes in handy, boy. It saves you a lot of hard work." Then it came out. He was sticking up harvest hands for their money. Once at a water tank and once in a boxcar he had pulled his gun and, "I pushed the gat into his guts and told him to come through with every dollar on him or I'd pull the trigger and he came through." I had thirty-odd dollars on me and was wondering why he didn't push the gat into my guts. I'm sure I would have come through with my last dollar. I think he still hoped I might buy a gun and go along with him as a partner. I left him when a freight came along. He said, "I expect some nice pickings here the next two or three days. Maybe I'll be seeing you in Rocky Ford on Melon Day."

Thousands poured into Rocky Ford for the Melon Day celebration. Watermelon and cantaloupe were handed out free. I rode a crowded passenger train that evening—sitting on a small board over the rods of a truck between the wheels. I changed for a freight train where I had a boxcar sleep and got off in the morning not knowing where I was. I didn't bother to go back and read the station sign. I ate a sandwich as I walked west on the railroad track. The day was sunny and cool. My eyes caught high rises of tumbling land I had never met before—the Rocky Mountains! Coming unexpectedly upon those rolling formations of rock and pine lifted away high, had me saying "There's the Hand of God." I couldn't think of anything before in my life that had me using that phrase.

I walked on to Canyon City, where I picked pears, earned meals and a few half-dollars, went on to Salida, where I spent two days and then took a Colorado Midland train heading back east, aiming for Denver. There wasn't an empty boxcar on the train, and for the first time I was riding the bumpers late at night. My feet were on the couplers between two cars and my hands were on the brake rod so in case my feet should slip I could hold on. Suddenly I was saying to myself, "You darn fool, you've been asleep." My numb brain was telling me that when you go to sleep on the bumpers you're in luck if your hands don't loosen and topple you down under the moving train. I would watch myself. But again I caught myself coming out of a sleep. From then on I wouldn't trust myself to be still for a second. I kept changing my position. I kept moving my feet and hands. I beat the sides of my head with a fist. I kicked one leg against the other. An hour of that and the train stopped. I got off and thanked God and the everlasting stars over the Rockies.

I saw Pikes Peak so I could say I saw it. At the Windsor, a first-class hotel in Denver, I washed dishes two weeks at a dollar and fifty cents a week, had a cubbyhole for a room, and meals as good as were served to the silk-hat guests. Then came the question, should I head for the West Coast or east to Galesburg? I admitted I was a little homesick. A passenger train was on slow speed out of the yards one night and I hopped on the steps of a Pullman vestibule. A conductor and porter ordered me off. I got off and saw the train slow to a stop. I climbed on top of a Pullman car, lay with my head toward the engine, and swore a solemn oath I wouldn't go to sleep. The car rocked and shook going around curves and my hands held tight so I wouldn't slide off. It was a cool September night and the train speed made it cold. I still had no underwear. I buttoned my coat, turned the collar up and tied a handkerchief around my neck. I went to sleep twice and coming out of it kept hitting and kicking myself to stay awake.

Daybreak came. An early farmer waved to me. I saw we were pulling in to a division point, McCook, Nebraska. I climbed down and started to walk out of the yards. A one-eyed man in plain clothes with a club and a star stood in my way. "Where did you come from?" His tone was horstyle. "I just got off that train," I said. He gave me orders in a more horstyle tone: "We don't want the likes of you in this town. You get back on that train." There were no trainmen in sight as I climbed back to where I had been riding. I had a daylight view of the Nebraska landscape for thirty miles from McCook to the next stop at Oxford. No one was waiting for me at Oxford. I went to a lunch counter, where they let me into the kitchen to wash off the cinders and soot. Then I ordered a monster thirty-five cent breakfast of ham and eggs, fried potatoes, bread, coffee, and two pieces of pie.

Heading east I stopped three days in a jungle with five good fellows. Shirt, socks, and handkerchiefs got washed. We had several meals of corn we picked from fields near by to roast or boil and sat around a fire talking after our supper. I caught a freight that landed me in Nebraska City. I chopped wood and picked apples for two sitdowns. At a large brick house where I chopped wood, the man of the house, a lawyer, seeing my suit of clothes somewhat ragged, asked me if I would like an old suit of his. He brought out an iron-gray all-wool suit, better than any I had had in my life. I offered to chop more wood but he laughed and said I'd better be on my way home. I found myself that night in a boxcar with four others. We spread newspapers under us, threw our coats over our shoulders, and tried for sleep. The night was clear and frosty. After a couple of hours we were saying, "It's too cold to sleep here." The five of us marched to the city calaboose and asked the marshal to let us in. The cells had the expected stink, but we spread our newspapers on the stone floor, slept warm, and on leaving were told to get out of town that day.

I caught a freight for Omaha. In Omaha, as in Kansas City and Denver, I stood before the United States Army recruiting office and read many times the pay and conditions Uncle Sam offered his Regular Army boys. I came near enlisting. One year of service I could see, or maybe two years, but the required three years had me backing out. I would make my decision, walk away, and come back the next day, read the pay and conditions and make the same decision that three years was too long.

The Hotel Mercer took me on as dishwasher at a dollar and fifty cents a week. The hotel was leased and run by a fancily dressed tall man who was known as Wink Taylor. I didn't notice him wink at any time but he probably had the name because he was quick as a wink. At the end of the first week I didn't get my pay nor at the end of the second week. Then came word that the Hotel Mercer was foreclosed and Wink Taylor vanished, owing me three dollars and owing the chambermaids, the dining-room and kitchen hands too.

I had one last sleep in the Mercer, crossed over to Council Bluff, had breakfast, then caught one freight train after another till I came in sight of Galesburg the afternoon of October fifteenth.

I walked along Berrien Street to the only house in the United States where I could open a door without knocking and walk in for a kiss from the woman of the house. They gave me a sitdown and as they had had only two or three letters from me, they asked questions about where I'd been. When I showed my father fifteen dollars and a few nickels, he said the money would come in handy and I should watch it. The clean bed sheets that night felt good.

Mart was suspicious of my fine suit of clothes. "I'll bet you didn't buy it new. If you bought it, it was a hockshop." So I told him how I got it. Mart said that along in August he had read in a newspaper about a hobo who fell off the bumpers in western Kansas and was mangled to death. The folks hadn't read it and he didn't tell them. "But I was afraid, Cully, that maybe it was you." Then I told him how in Colorado it could have been me.

What had the trip done to me? I couldn't say. It had changed me. I was easier about looking people in the eye. When questions came I was quicker at answering them or turning them off. I had been a young stranger meeting many odd strangers and I had practiced at having answers. At home and among my old chums of the Dirty Dozen they knew I had changed but they could no more tell how than I. Away deep in my heart now I had hope as never before. Struggles lay ahead, I was sure, but whatever they were I would not be afraid of them.

16

In the Army

I went to work on the Schwarz farm three miles east of Galesburg. I was up at four-thirty in the morning, curried two horses, and Mr. Schwarz and I milked twenty-two cows. I milked eight while Mr. Schwarz, older and faster, milked fourteen. We put the milk into eight-gallon cans and loaded them into a milk wagon. After breakfast I drove the milk into town and poured it out in pints and quarts. I bought a

Chicago Record every day and read in the wagon going back to the farm the two-column Home University series of lectures by University of Chicago professors on literature, history, politics, and government. The horses didn't mind. They liked going slow while I read.

After dinner I washed the cans and again Mr. Schwarz and I milked the cows. Mr. Schwarz was tall, somewhat stoop-shouldered, with a black beard—a kindly and gracious man, his people Pennsylvania Dutch. Mrs. Schwarz was robust, matronly, and when her fourteen-year-old daughter one evening at the supper table used the word "spondulix" she said sternly, "Why, Ethel, I'm surprised at you using such language." They were Methodists, well read, devout but not pious. You might have said they were a *Youth's Companion* family come true. Mrs. Schwarz had noticed that I spent the hour or two after supper reading among their books and magazines. She said to me one day with a beautifully serious look, "Charlie, I think you're going to make something of yourself." Until then Mary had been the only one to hand me anything like that. I was in bed every night at eight-thirty. I had come back to Galesburg weighing one hundred and thirty-six pounds and on the Schwarz farm I gained sixteen pounds.

About the middle of February I was sorry to leave the Schwarz home. I hired out to a blank-faced Swede to learn the painter's trade. At last it had come my way, a chance to learn a trade. A few of the ten-hour working days I was trusted to put on the first coat of paint. But most of the time I scraped and sandpapered. I climbed ladders outside of houses and stepladders inside and pushed sandpaper over wood to make it smooth for the painter. The boss was a man spare of words. My "Good morning" would bring a grunt from him. He believed in work without talk and toil without laughter. Once when he caught me singing his face had the look of a pickle fresh out of vinegar.

Each morning six days a week I was there at seven o'clock ready to wear out more sandpaper making more boards smooth for the boss and another painter. Not as much as a half-day a week did I swing a brush to put on a first coat. How long would this go on till they would let me put on a second and last coat?

On the night of February 15, 1898, I went to bed at nine-thirty. Not until later did I know that at two o'clock that morning the Secretary of the Navy in Washington heard a knock at the door that woke him and he was handed a telegram that nearly keeled him over. He got a White House watchman on the phone and told him to wake the President. On the phone Mr. McKinley heard the telegram read to him: "MAINE BLOWN UP IN HAVANA HARBOR AT NINE-FORTY TONIGHT. MANY WOUNDED AND DOUBTLESS MORE KILLED OR DROWNED." The *Maine* was a first-class battleship and of her three hundred and fifty-two officers and men, two hundred and sixty were dead and the ship had settled to the harbor bottom.

As the days went by and I went on sandpapering, I believed what I read and heard—that the same Spanish government whose General Weyler had killed thousands of Cuban patriots wanting independence and a republic had a hand in blowing up the *Maine*. I learned later that nobody knows how the *Maine* was exploded, whether some man did it or it was an act of God. I was going along with millions of other Americans who were about ready for a war to throw the Spanish government out of Cuba and let the people of Cuba have their republic. If a war did come, I knew what I would do. Across March and early April while the country roared with excite-ment, I went on sandpapering and thinking but I didn't tell my blank-faced boss what I was thinking.

President McKinley declared war and on April twenty-sixth I was sworn into Company C, Sixth Infantry Regiment of Illinois Volunteers, for two years of service. The regiment had been part of the

State Militia. Company C was a living part of Galesburg, had its drill hall, marched in uniform with
rifles and bayonets on public occasions, and went
to Springfield once a year for regimental maneuvers.
The company needed a dozen recruits to fill its quota
and I was among the earliest. I knew most of the
privates and had worked for Corporal Cully Rose at
the Auditorium. About three-fourths of the members
were from Galesburg and the rest from farms and
country towns around Galesburg. They elected their
own officers and you could hear fellows say, "No
West Pointers in this regiment."

When I quit my job and told the family I was
going to be a soldier they were sad and somewhat
puzzled, but they knew they couldn't stop me. Mart
spoke for the family, "We'd like the honor of having
a United States soldier in the family but we don't
want you to be killed." I said it might not be a real
war and if it was I might not get shot because some
soldiers always come back home. And besides, having seen the West I would now see the East and
maybe the Atlantic Ocean and Cuba. The family
were all there, with hundreds of other families, when
the train carrying Company C pulled out from the
Q. depot, now the "Burlington station."

On the fairgrounds at Springfield we were quartered in an immense brick building used for live-

stock exhibits. Where prize milk cows and blue-ribbon bulls had slept on straw we likewise had straw under our blankets in late April and early May. We were not lacking the lads who could moo like a Guernsey cow or bellow like a Holstein bull. While still in civilian clothes I was handed a Springfield rifle and put through the manual of arms and company drill.

In about ten days I slid into a uniform, a heavy blue-wool shirt, a coat of dark blue with brass buttons that went to the throat, pants of a light-blue wool cloth double as thick as the coat cloth. This was the same uniform the privates under Grant and Sherman had worn thirty-five years before, intended for wear in those border states of the South where snow fell and zero weather might come as at Fort Donelson the night Grant attacked. The little cap wouldn't shed rain from your ears, and above the stiff black visor it ran flat as though your head should be flat there. I felt honored to wear the uniform of famous Union armies and yet I had mistrust of it.

In a big room of the state capitol building a hundred of us passed before an examining surgeon, a German with a pronounced accent and a high falsetto voice. He was no stickler for regulations, this surgeon. When our friend Joe Dunn came he was found to be an inch or two short of the required height. The tears began running down Joe's face. The surgeon looked toward officers nearby and they gave him a nod. And he wrapped the measuring tape around a finger, measured again and found that Joe would pass.

We roamed around the capital, walked past the governor's house, out past the home of Abraham Lincoln. On the train to Washington rumors ran thick and fast about how soon we would be shooting Spaniards. On the day coaches we each had a wicker-covered seat to sit in and to take our night's sleep in. Canned beans, canned salmon, bread and coffee, were the rations. At some stations crowds met the train with cheers and smiles. The train arrived in Washington and the night was dark when it was shunted to Falls Church, Virginia. We marched two miles to level ground with underbrush and woods around it. We put up tents and slept on the ground, two soldiers to a tent. The next morning we went to the woods, cut saplings with crotched sticks and branches and made bunks to lay our blankets on.

I was in luck to have for a tent mate Andrew Tanning, as clean, scrupulous and orderly a corporal as ever served Uncle Sam. He was born in Sweden, had a prim face, a small mouth with a neat small mustache, and at no moment in our tent bunks at arm's length from each other did he ever let out one echo of a snore. Twice a week he wrote letters to his fine Swede girl in Galesburg whom he later married. Next to her he loved his Springfield rifle, and he kept it spotless. He took for himself the number of his rifle and would enter the tent saying, "Here comes Old Thirty-eight." He had belonged to Company C for two years and was a member of the Monarch Club, so I had danced with his sweetheart, Amanda Hanson, and her sister Tillie who was slim and in a waltz light as a white feather in a blue wind. Andy had been houseman of the Union Hotel when I was its barbershop porter. So we had plenty to talk about.

Across late May and all of June we drilled. We filled our canteens from a piped water supply and washed our shirts, socks, and underclothing at a murky creek in the woods. Most of the time we ate field rations as though we were in a campaign, bean soup and pork and beans more often than any other items. Our company cook—Arthur Metcalf, with his moon face and wide smiling mouth—was a prize. He did the best he could with what the War Department, through its quartermasters, let him have. I saw him one morning patiently cut away from a flitch of pork about a quarter of it that was alive with maggots. This was seven miles from the City of Washington where the Department of War had its office.

Our captain was Thomas Leslie McGirr, a second-rank Galesburg lawyer, a tall heavy man with a distinct paunch, heavy jaws, and a large mustache slightly graying. He kept by him a large yellow-haired St. Bernard dog named Smuggler, who in sight of the men was occasionally fed juicy sirloin steaks. Our first lieutenant was Conrad Byloff, my classmate in the Seventh Ward school, who had learned the boilermaker's trade working for the Q. His father had been a captain in the Swedish army, and Con himself seemed to be a born commander. The men had depths of affection for him; he could be stern giving commands, but he never drilled us without giving us a smile that said we could get fun out of what we were doing. Our second lieutenant was Daniel K. Smyth, a scholar and a gentleman ever considerate of his men.

Of the nine sergeants and eleven corporals I couldn't think of one I hated. How can you possibly forget a first sergeant who trains his voice every day by six and eight times calling off a hundred names? After a few weeks some of the men without looking in a book could call the roll from Benjamin Anderson to Henry Clay Woodward as smoothly as F. Elmer

Johnson, first sergeant, who kept records, read orders, and was the hardest-worked man in the company. Corporal Ed Peckenpaugh was up and down the company street and only the hard of hearing failed to get his baritone giving out "I Guess I'll Have to Telegraph My Baby." Corporal James Switzer was the company bugler, a handsome boy of seventeen, nicknamed "Mim."

Ten of our company were Knox students and two were from Lombard; twenty or more were farm boys. At least twenty had had fathers, uncles, or near kinsmen in the Civil War. All had mixed motives in enlisting. Love of adventure, or a curiosity about facing dangers and standing hardships was one and, I would judge, the outstanding one. A mystic love of country and the flag was there in degree among most of the men. Breaking away from a monotonous home environment to go where there was excitement could be read in the talk of some fellows. At least two of the older men had troublesome wives at home. The hope of pensions after service was sometimes definitely mentioned. Over all of us in 1898 was the shadow of the Civil War and the men who fought it to the end that had come only thirty-three years before our enlistment. Our motives were as mixed as theirs. In the lonely hours of guard duty you could study about why you had enlisted.

On leave for a day we walked two miles to Falls Church, took a trolley to Washington, saw the Capitol and walked past the White House. I had my first look at the Ford Theatre outside and inside and the outside of the Peterson House across the street.

For our State Militia caps we got felt hats with wide brims, and to replace our Springfield rifles we were issued Krag-Jörgensens. July sixth saw hustling and gabble. We began riding an Atlantic Coast Line train across Virginia and North Carolina to Charleston, South Carolina. We had our first look at tobacco and cotton growing, at the mansions, cabins, and hovels of the South, and at stations here and there men selling bottles of "cawn lickah" that had the color of rain water. We slept overnight in our coach seats and the next day quartered in big cotton warehouses on the wharf. We went swimming next to the wharf, and you could see the Illinois prairie boys taking mouthfuls of Atlantic Ocean water to taste it, then calling to each other, "It *is* salt, isn't it?" As we strolled around Charleston in our Civil War uniforms, the people were warmhearted and cordial. Restaurants and saloons refused to take our money for what they served us. Negroes stood quietly to one side and took off their hats to us. We had been issued hardtack, tough and flat biscuits that were as good as money. On a dare, a southern belle gave one of our boys a big resounding kiss for one hardtack.

We saw lying at anchor the *Rita*, a lumber-hauling freighter, the first ship our navy had captured from the Spanish. Six companies of the Sixth Illinois boarded her on July eleventh, each man given a bunk made of new rough lumber. Running your bare arm or leg over it, you met splinters. The air below was heavy, warm, and humid. On clear nights several hundred men brought their blankets up and covered the upper deck as they slept. The first day out one man said, "This tub rolls like a raw egg in a glass of whisky." One of the seasick said to another, "Why is your face so lemon-green?" The rations were mostly cold canned beans and canned salmon. The day or two when canned tomatoes were issued we called holidays. The band played every day and men were thankful. A waterspout was sighted one day, one shark and a few flying fish another day, and the landlubbers felt this was part of what they had come for.

The *Rita* arrived in Guantánamo Bay, Cuba, on the evening of July seventeenth, our band playing and cheers coming to us from the decks of famous battleships, the *Oregon*, the *Indiana*, the *Iowa*, and more cheers from cruisers and torpedo boats. In the morning Colonel Jack Foster and staff officers went ashore and came back soon with word that Santiago was taken and we wouldn't be put ashore to fight in Cuba. Some men were disappointed; others were satisfied. Also, it was reported, there were ashore some four hundred troop cases of yellow fever and Colonel Jack had been ordered to get back to the *Rita* at once.

We lay at anchor a few days, and when we sailed out of Guantánamo Bay, rumors ran that we were going to Porto Rico. If we had been reading United States newspapers, we would have believed we were going to land at Cape Fajardo near San Juan, the capital of Porto Rico. But about halfway to Porto Rico, General Nelson A. Miles, commander of the three thousand men in this expedition, changed his mind. Instead of landing at Cape Fajardo on the north coast we would land on the south coast of Porto Rico. The idea came to him that since the War Department had told the newspapers and the newspapers had told the world where his expedition was going to land and march and fight it might be safer and easier to land somewhere else where he wasn't expected. There were those who said afterward that to attack the fortified harbor of San Juan would have required the navy and the guns of the fleet and General Miles as an army man preferred to land on the south coast and have the army take over the island from the south so that in time San Juan wouldn't have much of an island to govern. We heard later too that the Secretary of War and many others in the United States were stupefied to learn that General Miles had changed his mind and begun operations on the south coast.

Soon after daylight on July twenty-fifth we sighted a harbor and moved into it. Ahead we saw gunfire from a ship and landing boats filled with blue-jackets moving toward shore. We were ordered to put on our cartridge belts and with rifles get into full marching outfits. We heard shooting, glanced toward shore and saw white puffs of smoke while we stood waiting our turns to climb down rope ladders into long boats called lighters. We were rowed to a shallow beach where we dropped into water above our hips. Holding rifles over our heads, we waded ashore.

We were in Guánica, a one-street town with palm and coconut trees new to us. We expected to be ordered into action against Spanish troops somewhere in the town or nearby hills. We were marched to a field near the town where we waited over noon and afternoon. We ate our supper of cold canned beans and hardtack and soon were ordered to march. When we came to a halt we waited in the dark and heard shots that seemed not far away. This was the one time on that island when most of us expected to go into battle. And it didn't happen. We waited and marched back to our field near Guánica.

In the morning we marched to Yauco and on to Ponce, finding those towns surrendered. We camped in a wooded ravine two nights. After the first two or three hours of mosquito bites, sleeping in our underwear and barefoot, we put on our pants, wool shirts, and socks, for all of the moist heat. They were large, ravenous, pitiless mosquitoes. "They came with bugles sounding mess call," said one man with a swollen face. I had one eye closed by the swellings around it. Some fellows had both eyes closed. On the second night I followed others in wrapping my rubber poncho around my head. After an hour I would wake with an aching head from foul air breathed over too many times. I would throw the poncho off, beat away the mosquitoes, wrap the poncho around my head again, then sleep till awakening with a headache—and repeat.

On roads and streets as we marched were barefooted men and women smiling and calling to us *"Puerto Rico Americano."* For four hundred years this island had been run by a Spanish government at Madrid. Now it was to be American and it was plain that the island common people liked the idea and had more hope of it. More than once we saw on the roadside a barefoot man wearing only pants, shirt, and hat, eating away at an ear of parched corn. We saw knee-high children wearing only a ragged shirt, and their little swollen bellies told of not enough food and not the right kind.

We camped at Ponce a few days and then began a march up mountain roads. The August tropic heat was on. We carried cartridge belt, rifle, bayonet, blanket roll, half a canvas pup tent, haversack with rations, a coat. We still wore the heavy blue-wool pants of the '65 Army of the Potomac and thick canvas leggings laced from ankles to knees. On one halt after another there were men tearing their blankets in two so as to lessen weight to carry. I tore a third of mine away. Some let the whole blanket go. Men fell out, worn out, and there were sunstroke cases. It was an eight-mile march upgrade. We halted for the night on a slope above the road. We were sleeping and all was quiet about midnight. Suddenly came a shriek. Then a series of yells and shrieks and several companies of men were rushing headlong down the slope to the road. Men sleeping or just awakened were trampled and bruised. It was found that one of the bullocks hauling carts loaded with supplies and ammunition had got loose and hunting for grass had tramped on a sleeper who gave the first piercing shriek that was taken up by others. We went up the slope and back to our sleep calling it the "First Battle of Bull Run."

We camped on a slope on the edge of Adjuntas, where we saw the American flag run up. Cook Metcalf over a long afternoon had boiled a tinned beef we named "Red Horse." For all the boiling it was stringy and tasteless. We set up our pup tents, laid our ponchos and blankets on the ground, and went to sleep in a slow drizzle of rain. About three o'clock in the morning there was a heavy downpour that kept up, and the downhill water soaked our blankets. We got out of our tents, wrung our blankets as dry as we could and threw them with ponchos over our shoulders. Then a thousand men stood around waiting for daylight and hoping the rain would let up. When daylight came Metcalf managed some hot pork and beans with coffee. Midmorning the sun came out and we dried and marched on to Utuado.

There at Utuado came news, "The protocol has been signed and peace is declared and we are ordered back to Ponce." Marching down the mountain roads we had climbed came easy along with rumors that we would take transports home from Ponce. We were lighthearted and cried, "Hurrah for the protocol!" It was a new funny word we liked. We slept a night in a building used for drying coffee. Each man fitted nicely into a dry bin enclosure rich with a coffee smell.

At Ponce many of us weighed to see what we had sweated and groaned out. All but a half-dozen men had lost weight. The scales said my one hundred and fifty-two pounds in April had gone down to one hundred and thirty pounds in August. Many were gaunt and thin, with a slightly yellow tint on the skin. Uniforms were fading, here and there ragged and torn. Hats had holes in them.

Our transport with the whole Sixth Illinois sailed for New York. We were divided into messes of eight men for rations. A tin of "Red Horse" would be handed to one man who opened it. He would put it to his nose, smell of it, wrinkle up his face, and take a spit. The next man would do the same, and the next till the eight men of the mess had smelled, grimaced, and spit. Then that tin of "Red Horse" was thrown overboard for any of the fishes of the Atlantic Ocean who might like it. Somehow we got along on cold canned beans, occasional salmon, and the reliable hardtack. What we called "Red Horse" soon had all of the country scandalized with its new name of "Embalmed Beef."

On the transport we went through a ceremonial we had gone through many times before. A circle of men might be sitting on deck talking and jollying when one would call out "Shirts off! Time for inspection!" Then each man would run his eyes over all parts of the shirt, especially the seams, pick off the gray backs and crush them. Underwear and pants were more of a problem. In camp we boiled them occasionally when there was time and a big kettle of water.

When Richard Harding Davis wrote that for the troops under General Miles "Porto Rico was a picnic" he was remembering he had lived with the high commanding officers. When he wrote, "In comparison to the Santiago nightmare, the Porto Rican expedition was a *fête des fleurs*," he was writing sober and awful historical fact. But only by comparison with that nightmare of blood, fever, and blunders was our campaign a feast of flowers. Mud and mosquitoes are not roses and poinsettias. Nor is sleeping in rain and marching in a baking sun carrying fifty pounds a feast. Few are the picnics where they eat from baskets holding canned beans, hardtack, and "Red Horse" and then take off their shirts and pluck out "seam squirrels." The war, though a small one, was the first in which the United States sent troops on ocean transports to fight on foreign soil and acquire island possessions. It was a small war edging toward immense consequences.

We sailed into the port of New York at night, docked at Weehawken, and in the morning saw a small crowd waving at us. On the dock I bought a loaf of white bread for a nickel and a quart of milk for another nickel. As I ate that bread and milk I felt that I had been an animal and was now a human being—it was so clean, tasty, delicious. We were in the newspapers, and as we roamed around New York City, men and women stopped us to ask where we had been, some to ask if we had news of regiments their boys were in, others to ask what we might want in the way of food or drink. People saw we looked lean, somewhat faded and ragged, tanned by sun and sea, hard-bitten by circumstances and insects. There was hospitality that made us feel good about the country. They acted like we were heroes. We had our doubts about that but we did know we could use more fresh victuals and boiling hot water with strong soap. At moments you just had to reach in to scratch at an armpit.

Again in a train of coaches with wicker seats we rode and slept, reached Springfield, Illinois, and camped there while our muster-out papers were arranged. When our train pulled into the Burlington station at Galesburg on September twenty-first we had been gone only five months but we looked like we had been somewhere. The station platform swarmed with a crowd that overran Seminary Street for a block to the north, and from there on to Main Street the sidewalks were thick with people. I caught my mother's face and others of the family laughing and waving their hands high. We made a company formation and marched to the Company C drill hall.

I went that evening with Mary to a farmhouse near Dahinda where she was teaching a country school. They put me in a room with a four-poster feather bed, and I sank into the feathers for a sleep. I tossed around a half-hour, then got out of the bed and in thirty seconds went to sleep on the rag carpet on the floor.

The next day I went home. Mart said, "Well, you didn't get killed, did you?" "No, they didn't give me a chance." "What did you learn?" Mart went on. "I learnt more than I can use." "Well," said Mart, "last year you were a hobo and this year a soldier. What's next with you?" "Maybe I'll go to college." "College! That'll be something!"

My father gave me a rich smile and a handshake that wilted me. He said he stayed on the job the day before and when shopmen asked why he didn't take the day off, he said, "I will see my boy at home and he will tell me everything." Mother said it had been a big summer for him, with the shopmen and neighbors often asking, "How's the boy, Gus?" or,

"Company C is getting a long ways from home, Gus. We hope your boy comes through all right." Mart told me such talk hit our old man deep and it seemed that now he was sure he was an Americanized citizen. I gave him fifty dollars of my muster-out money, which came to one hundred and three dollars and seventy-three cents in all.

We were in the newspapers that week. The Army and Navy League gave us a banquet at the Universalist Church and the Ladies' Society of the First Presbyterian Church another big dinner. The biggest affair was an oyster supper in the basement of the First Methodist Church where ex-Mayor Forrest F. Cooke, Congressman George W. Prince, and the Reverend W. H. Geistweit spoke. President Finley of Knox read a poem about our exploits—a freegoing poem with nice touches of humor, and a printed copy of it in a little book with red covers was presented to each member of Company C.

In nearly every life come sudden little events not expected that change its course. Two such events came for me. Private George R. Longbrake of Company C, whose backyard on Brooks Street touched our backyard on Berrien, had spoken to me on the transport about my going to Lombard, now a university, where he had been a student for a year. He asked whether I would enter if, as he believed, they would give me free tuition for a year. I said yes. So after all the cheering and the church banquets were over, he came to me to say the arrangement had been cheerfully made at Lombard. Private Lewis W. Kay, one of the two Lombard students in Company C, had died of fever about the time of our muster-out.

Then came Wiz Brown saying there was a fire-department job vacant. The department had two "call men" who slept at the firehouse at night and reported by telephone in the daytime if the fire whistle blew. If it was a big fire they bicycled to it as fast as their pedals would take them. A call man was paid ten dollars a month. "That's nice money, Cully, and I'm sure if I speak to Mayor Carney he'll appoint you," said Wiz. He appointed me. I bought a bicycle and a blue shirt with two rows of pearl buttons of silver-dollar size and a big collar that buttoned far down the chest. I began sleeping on the second floor of the Prairie Street firehouse. We were sixteen men sleeping in one room. Alongside each iron frame bed was a pair of rubber boots with pants and when the alarm bell rang we stepped out of bed, pulled up the pants, ran to slide down a brass pole and hop on the chemical wagon or the hose cart. Chief Jim O'Brien gave me a glad hand and said, "Considering where you've been, Charlie, I think you'll make a good fireman."

I enrolled at Lombard for classes in Latin, English, inorganic chemistry, elocution, drama, and public speaking. They had an "elective system," and that was what I elected. In a few days I would report at eight o'clock in the morning for a class in Latin under Professor Jon W. Grubb. Years back I had seen him milk a cow and drive her to pasture. I thought it would be interesting to study Caesar's *Commentaries* with a professor who could wear overalls and milk a cow. I would have to leave class when the fire whistle blew but that wasn't often enough to bother either the class or the professor.

I was going to get an education. I remembered Lottie Goldquist saying you could never get enough of it.

Have you read these Odyssey Classics?

Edward Eager
HALF MAGIC
KNIGHT'S CASTLE
MAGIC BY THE LAKE
MAGIC OR NOT?
SEVEN-DAY MAGIC
THE TIME GARDEN
THE WELL-WISHERS

L. M. Boston
THE CHILDREN OF GREEN KNOWE
TREASURE OF GREEN KNOWE
THE RIVER AT GREEN KNOWE
A STRANGER AT GREEN KNOWE
AN ENEMY AT GREEN KNOWE

Mary Norton
BED-KNOB AND BROOMSTICK
THE BORROWERS
THE BORROWERS AFIELD
THE BORROWERS AFLOAT
THE BORROWERS ALOFT
THE BORROWERS AVENGED

John R. Tunis
THE KID FROM TOMKINSVILLE
WORLD SERIES
KEYSTONE KIDS
ROOKIE OF THE YEAR
YEA! WILDCATS!
A CITY FOR LINCOLN
IRON DUKE
THE DUKE DECIDES
ALL-AMERICAN
CHAMPION'S CHOICE

Eleanor Estes
GINGER PYE
THE WITCH FAMILY

William O. Steele
THE BUFFALO KNIFE
FLAMING ARROWS
THE PERILOUS ROAD
WINTER DANGER

Carolyn Haywood
"B" IS FOR BETSY
BETSY AND BILLY
BACK TO SCHOOL WITH BETSY
BETSY AND THE BOYS

Carl Sandburg
PRAIRIE-TOWN BOY
ROOTABAGA STORIES, PART ONE
ROOTABAGA STORIES, PART TWO

Carol Kendall
THE GAMMAGE CUP

Virginia Sorensen
MIRACLES ON MAPLE HILL

Henry Winterfeld
CASTAWAYS IN LILLIPUT
DETECTIVES IN TOGAS
MYSTERY OF THE ROMAN RANSOM
TROUBLE AT TIMPETILL

Elizabeth Enright
GONE-AWAY LAKE
RETURN TO GONE-AWAY

Anne Holm
NORTH TO FREEDOM

Milton Meltzer
UNDERGROUND MAN

Look for Odyssey Classics in your local bookstore.
To order directly from HBJ, call 1-800-543-1918 (ask for Operator J).

Printed in the United States
137064LV00001B/46/A